THE CURIOUS CASE OF THE MAYO LIBRARIAN

THE CURIOUS CASE OF THE MAYO LIBRARIAN

Pat Walsh

MERCIER PRESS

WHAT YOU NEED TO READ

MERCIER PRESS

Cork

www. mercierpress.ie

Trade enquiries to CMD,
55A Spruce Avenue, Stillorgan Industrial Park,
Blackrock, County Dublin

© Pat Walsh, 2009

ISBN: 978 1 85635 615 2

10 9 8 7 6 5 4 3 2 1

A CIP record for this title is available from the British Library

 Mercier Press receives financial assistance from the Arts
Council/An Chomhairle Ealaíon

Printed and bound in the EU.

Contents

Acknowledgements

I would like to thank Shelley Healy, Ciara Jones, Fionnuala Carton, Patricia Byrne, Geraldine McHugh, Eithne Prout and all the staff of Dún Laoghaire-Rathdown Libraries for their help and patience while I've been researching this book. Rev. Dudley Levinstone Cooney and Rev. Robin Roddie of the Wesley Historical Society of Ireland, Alun Bevan of Comhairle Leabharlanna, Marian Keyes of the Library Association, Terry Wogan of Ballyfermot Library, the staff of the Military Archives and the staff of UCD Archives Department were also very generous with their time and effort. The National Library, the Director and staff of the National Archives and Mayo County Libraries should also be acknowledged.

Thanks also to Eoin Purcell, Wendy Logue and Patrick Crowley of Mercier Press.

Introduction

'A free fight in County Mayo'

By early afternoon on Saturday, 27 December 1930, a large and boisterous crowd had gathered in the public gallery of the council chamber of Castlebar courthouse. They had come to attend a special meeting of Mayo County Council. Much controversy had been stirred up in Mayo in the previous weeks over the issue of who was to be appointed the next county librarian. Despite the scheduling of the meeting in the middle of the Christmas holiday period, the sizeable gathering was determined to show its concern.

In many ways the atmosphere was similar to that at a football match. As the correspondent of the *Roscommon Herald* put it, 'How humorously inconsistent is this latest "crisis" then, for it originated in the act of a deceased Scotch millionaire, old Andrew Carnegie, who, when he conceived the benevolent idea of presenting free libraries in these countries, never dreamt that he would provoke a free fight in County Mayo.'[1]

Miss Letitia Dunbar Harrison was a graduate of Trinity College and a Protestant. In July 1930 she had been successful at interview for the vacant post of Mayo county librarian. Mayo County Council's library committee refused to endorse her appointment and subsequently a full meeting of the council also rejected her. The reason they gave was that she did not have sufficient knowledge of the Irish language.

The Cumann na nGaedheal government, led by the President of the Executive Council, William T. Cosgrave (the equivalent of the present-day taoiseach), and the Minister for Local Government, Richard Mulcahy, or General Mulcahy as he was widely known at the time even though he was no longer a member of the army, insisted that the recommendation of the Local Appointments Commission (LAC) be enforced and that Miss Dunbar Harrison be employed. The County Council maintained their resistance. A tense stand-off ensued, with each side waiting to see if the other would be the first to back down.

News of 'the Mayo library row', as it became popularly known, was not confined to the county. Not only did it make headlines in Ireland, but it also caught the attention of newspapers in places as far away as Boston and London, mainly among the immigrant Irish population.[2] The assembled multitude in Castlebar were aware of the background to the crisis and that the special meeting had been convened with Mayo County Council under threat of abolition. For many this aspect of local politics was merely a spectator sport. As the *Roscommon Herald* put it, 'Even if they could not observe the peace and goodwill part of the Christmas tradition towards "Dick Mulcahy", as they called the Minister for Local Government and those who supported his "brow-beating", still they were not going to let that spoil the festive side of the season.'[3]

The *Irish Independent* reported that 'the proceedings and the discussion, which was throughout lively and occasionally acrimonious, was keenly followed by a crowded and at times noisy gallery, the occupants of which sent up spirals of pipe and cigarette smoke which at times seemed to challenge the illuminative power of the Shannon [electricity] in the chamber.'[4]

Outside, an orchestra of optimistic Wren Boys from Ballina tried in vain to make themselves heard above the rumblings of a howling gale. Local amusements at this time of year were scarce so the crowd was in a festive mood. According to the *Roscommon Herald*, the entertainment provided by the Wren Boys, who were grotesquely costumed and had a limited repertoire, held the crowd's interest for only 'a short period at any time, but when it is kept up for a week it is small wonder that any other little diversion is welcome.'[5]

Inside the courthouse the crowd were in high spirits. Forecasts of the result of the voting, which proved to be 'remarkably accurate' according to the *Irish Independent*, were passed around during the debate along with 'clever Limericks', many of them 'amusingly explanatory of the attitude of certain persons towards the appointment of Miss Dunbar.'[6]

The *Roscommon Herald* gave its account of events under the headline, 'Drama and Comedy at Mayo County Council Meeting'. The paper asserted that 'if the oratory of Mayo's elected representatives, which we listened to for three hours in the council chamber in Castlebar on Saturday, be a true index of local sentiment, the people of that part of Connaught are ardent disciples of "Ourselves Alone".'[7]

The meeting began promptly at 1 p.m. under the chairmanship of Pat Higgins. He stood in for the County Council chairman, Michael Davis, also a TD for Mayo North and a senior member of the Cumann na nGaedheal Party, who had refused to attend. In fact Michael Davis had declined to have anything to do with the meeting. Out of a possible thirty-eight councillors, twenty-seven were in attendance. The majority of the absentee councillors were of the Cumann na nGaedheal persuasion.

The office of Mayo county librarian was hardly a crucial post. It was normally little more than a routine appointment, yet its filling had escalated into a conflict that had national consequences. It had pitted church against state, county council against government department and even members of the same political party against each other. Most of Cumann na nGaedheal's local politicians were very unhappy with what they saw as their own party's obdurate stance on the issue.

The crisis began with a dispute over the filling of a minor post, but the quarrel spread so rapidly that it now called into the question the continued existence of Mayo County Council. Such was the heat generated by the dispute and so fundamental were the issues it raised, particularly in the area of church-state relations, that it could even have brought down the Cumann na nGaedheal government. And all over one small job in Mayo.

Investigating the background to the squabble uncovers many of the fault-lines of the newly formed Free State. Examining the anatomy of the crisis lays bare the tensions of society in 1930s Ireland as it moved away from colonial rule. These tensions were all the more obvious given that the dispute was over a relatively trivial local appointment.

Chapter 1

'Chuck the library'

The first inklings of trouble came to light on 1 November 1930. In a short article in *The Connaught Telegraph* it was reported that, at a meeting held in Castlebar courthouse, the County Council's library committee had rejected the recommendation of the Local Appointments Commission to appoint Miss Dunbar Harrison as Mayo county librarian, on the grounds that she did not have the requisite knowledge of Irish. The proceedings were held in private with the newspaper merely reporting the outcome in a few succinct paragraphs.[1] The Local Appointments Commission was the independent body set up by the Cumann na nGaedheal government to oversee the recruitment of senior posts in the local authorities.

When the library committee's decision was brought up before the full meeting of the council, a letter from the Department of Local Government was read aloud. It stated that the council had no choice but to appoint Miss Dunbar Harrison. The county secretary, M.J. Egan, suggested that it be referred back to the library committee without further discussion. Councillor Waldron objected, stating that he had been against the library all along due to the cost. Michael Davis, the chairman of the council, called him to order, but Councillor Waldron persisted. 'Chuck the library and you will require no librarian,' he proposed.[2] Eventually it was agreed to accept Mr Egan's suggestion and the matter was referred back to the library committee for further consideration.

Rev. Naughton, Bishop of Killala, presided over the next meeting of the Mayo County Council library committee, which was held in Castlebar courthouse on Monday, 30 November. The sole matter on the agenda was to consider both the recommendation of the Local Appointments Commission to appoint Miss Dunbar Harrison and the subsequent letter from the Department of Local Government calling on them to endorse the recommendation.

Due to the widespread local interest in the matter, on the proposal of Councillor Moclair the meeting was, for the first time, held in public. Councillor Moclair's initiative also ensured that the debate was widely covered in the local and national press.

Attending the meeting were:

> Rev. Dr Naughton, Bishop of Killala, chair of the meeting
> Archdeacon Fallon, Castlebar
> Canon Hegarty, Belmullet
> Dean D'Alton, Ballinrobe
> Rev. Higgins, Bohola
> Brother Kelly, Westport
> Rev. Prendergast, Castlebar
> Rev. Jackson (Rector), Castlebar
> Dr Anthony McBride
> Councillor T.S. Moclair
> Councillor Bernard Joyce
> Councillor Pat Higgins

As is obvious from this list, the committee was very much dominated by the clergy. A head (or collar) count shows that it was made up of one bishop, five priests, one Christian Brother, one Protestant rector and four laymen. This would not have been all that unusual at the time, as men of the cloth were regarded as having an occupational interest in libraries. Book selection was something that had to be monitored carefully. If one was not careful, libraries could easily become occasions of sin.

Mayo library committee had a much larger potential attendance of thirty-eight members. However, many of these were infrequent attendees. The clergy were generally the most diligent members. It was an all-male committee, which was again not uncommon at the time. Mayo County Council was also an all-male assembly. On the other hand, many women were avid readers and a significant proportion of county librarians were female. Librarianship was seen as a genteel profession, a suitable occupation for a woman.

Mr M.J. Egan, the county secretary, and Mr A. Hamrock, acting librarian, were also in attendance in an advisory capacity. Mr Egan conducted the proceedings and read the minutes of the previous meeting, which had been forwarded to the ministry and submitted to a full meeting of the County Council. Mr Egan then read into the minutes of the meeting the letter from the Department of Local Government. The contents of this letter were to the effect that the appointment of Miss Dunbar Harrison would be insisted upon.

'That is now the situation,' Mr Egan concluded.

Dean Edward D'Alton, PP, Ballinrobe, rose and proposed that they simply adhere to the resolution passed on the previous occasion. 'First of all Miss Dunbar is not fully qualified,' he claimed, before adding, 'They have taken very good care not to give us the names of the candidates who presented themselves or the marks given. In Ballinrobe some years ago we had a girl who taught commercial subjects, but because she could not teach through the medium of Irish she could not be sanctioned. [Yet] if she used Irish she would have no students as they couldn't follow the instruction in Irish. For every single position it was the same – nurses, doctors, and even mid-wives had to know Irish. I believe if a carpenter looks for a job he must know it and if a farrier looks for the shoeing of horses he must know it too. It's a wonder they do not require the horse to know it.'[3]

Laughter greeted his remark.

'That is the case and now we are asked to turn around and appoint a girl who knows no Irish. The County Mayo is scheduled in the Gaeltacht, but it is ridiculous to say everyone in it speaks Irish. It is equally ridiculous that in the districts where the people speak nothing but Irish that no effort should be made to help them, so that it is obvious that the person appointed should have Irish.'

'We are not appointing a washerwoman or a mechanic'

'I would like to know,' Dean D'Alton continued, 'what chance a Catholic girl would have if she went to Belfast to get a position like this? The proportion of Catholics in Belfast is not as great as in this county, but I suppose quarter of the population of Belfast is Catholic. North of the Boyne, there is a Protestant ascendancy and a most aggressive, impudent ascendancy they are. We are asked to set up a Protestant ascendancy in Mayo, a hundred years after Catholic Emancipation and every vestige of the Penal Laws wiped out. We are not appointing a washerwoman or a mechanic where religion would not come in, but an educated girl who should be able to estimate the value of the books to be put into the hands of the boys and girls of Mayo.'[4]

Dean D'Alton then mentioned the recently concluded Lambeth Conference, a congress of the Anglican church that had debated such issues as birth control and trial marriages. It had given conditional approval for the use of contraceptives in certain cases. This was, of course, anathema to the Catholic church.

'Is it fair,' asked Dean D'Alton, 'that a girl, a non-Catholic not in sympathy with Catholic views but those of the Protestant clergy, should be appointed librarian to County Mayo? The minister can enforce this appointment. It is evident he intends to force the girl on us. It would be a curious thing to do. I think he will have public opinion strongly against him. I think he will find it a pyrrhic victory, but it will be a great deal better for him to take defeat. He will have to face the electors. I will oppose the appointment in as far as I can, as I do not think her a fit and proper person to be appointed and if there is only myself here I will continue the opposition as far as I can.'[5]

As Dean D'Alton took his seat, Councillor Bernard Joyce and Canon Hegarty rose simultaneously. Councillor Joyce having made the first utterance, Canon Hegarty sat back down. Councillor Joyce proceeded. He said he wished to second the proposition but not for the same reasons that Dean D'Alton had outlined.

'Personally,' he declared, 'I do not approve of the system of appointments now in vogue. It is not a recommendation in the strict sense of the word but rather a mandate to be obeyed. As I understand it, it is more in the line of dictation than a recommendation to the representatives of the county.'

Councillor Joyce went on to mention a disagreement that had arisen between the County Council and the Department of Local Government over the appointment of a county medical officer. 'Now I think the council has cleared the air very much in that respect,' he said, 'and the people of Mayo should stand a little more together with regard to local affairs in their own county … The Dean pointed out that only the name of a non-Catholic was mentioned. He did not wish to hurt the feelings of anyone. Neither do I, but it stands to reason that it is not a recommendation but a mandate. The young lady suggested may be all right, but I do not think her appointment would mean the success of the library in Mayo and I have pleasure in seconding the proposition that she be not appointed. If appointed by us, I can assure you that she will not be accepted by the County Council.'[6]

Canon Hegarty then got his chance to speak. He rose to support the proposition. 'I intend to develop the arguments put forward,' he said. 'Our religion was persecuted because our politics were Irish and national, and the politics of Mayo are today national and Irish and it is extraordinary that it rests with an Irish national government to select a West Briton to cater for the political, the literary, the economic, the religious and the moral interests of the people of Mayo and for the 99 per cent who are Catholic. Now it rests with an Irish national government to send us a young lady for whom I have not the slightest blame. She is looking for a position. I cannot blame her. But undoubtedly the people who have assigned her to Catholic and nationalist Mayo have made a very serious mistake. The business of government is to promote the good of the community, to fall in with the general idea of the country.

'Cromwell came to this country and our ancestors had no option but to go "to Hell or to Connacht" to make room for a class that was not of our race or religion and now a national government has given the people the option of becoming West Britons or going into the mountains and glens again and leave knowledge aside in order to preserve what they hold most dear. A librarian is a teacher. She has to deal with books that are designed to give instruction, education and amusement. Therefore you will allow, whatever class they may be, they will leave a trace behind them.'[7]

Canon Hegarty went on to refer to the previous county librarian and a disagreement that she'd had with the Department of Local Government. He added that he had received letters from other potential female candidates for the position, all of whom had ample Irish. He also questioned why the age qualification had been raised from twenty-one to twenty-five years of age.[8]

Dr Anthony McBride, a brother of Major John McBride, who had been executed after the 1916 Rising, then spoke in favour of the appointment. 'I propose that Miss Dunbar be appointed,' he said. 'There is no law in the Constitution of the Irish Free State against Protestants or graduates of Trinity College or any citizens of the state being appointed to any position in it, provided they are qualified. Trinity College turned out some of the greatest Irishmen the world has seen. It is recognised the world over as an Irish university. I cannot assume or accept that the Local Appointments Commission were not honest in making the selection. We are bound to accept their decision.' He then pointed out that successful candidates who did not have Irish had three years in which to acquire a passable knowledge of it.

'I stand by the Constitution'

'I think it would be an abominable thing,' Dr McBride continued, 'if we did not carry out the Constitution made by Irishmen for

Ireland and the Irish people, and that every Irish citizen, no matter of what colour, of what class, of what creed, should have equal chance in securing the appointments in it. The committee has no discretion on the matter, the system of appointment having been accepted. This young lady was found to be the best qualified, except that she did not have a full knowledge of Irish. It would be an awful thing to take the question of religion into consideration. We had religious persecution in former days and we should not continue that on our own side now. I need say no more. I stand by the Constitution on this question.'[9]

Rev. Jackson seconded Dr McBride's proposal to support the Local Appointments Commission's recommendation. He was of the impression that the County Council had invited the LAC to do what was necessary to fill the post.

'I think it would be a great acquisition to the county,' he said, 'to have a young lady who is so well qualified as a librarian ... Reference was made to sending her north of the Boyne. What an effect it would have on people north of the border if it went forth to the world that Mayo library committee had appointed a Protestant and a graduate of Trinity College to this responsible position. We want to unite the North and the South and what an effect it would have for broad-mindedness and tolerance in this part of the country if we here in Mayo appointed Miss Dunbar.'[10]

Mr Egan, the county secretary, corrected Rev. Jackson's explanation of the role of the Local Appointments Commission. He pointed out that the implementation of the recommendations received was not optional, but in fact compulsory. The Local Appointments Commission had been set up by the government to oversee the filling of such positions as county librarian. Rev. Jackson accepted the correction. Councillor Moclair said that he was glad that the county secretary had corrected Rev. Jackson as it saved him from doing so. He then spoke up in favour of Dean D'Alton's motion.

'Talk to the vegetables better and make the cows work overtime'

'The government are blowing hot and cold in regard to Irish,' he said. 'One time they are going madly for it and another time madly against it. At the mental hospital they compelled the farm steward to have a knowledge of Irish so he could talk to the vegetables better and make the cows work overtime.'[11]

Again laughter greeted his remark.

Brother Kelly was next to speak. In his opinion Miss Dunbar Harrison was not a fit subject to be appointed librarian in Mayo. He believed her mental outlook and constitution was the self-same outlook and mental constitution of Trinity College. He believed that this anti-Irish institution had an evil history as far as Ireland and the Irish people were concerned and there was no sign of this altering to any extent. The college had been endowed for 330 years by the government of England and, during that time, never ceased to regard itself as alien and hostile to Irish aspirations, culture and customs. He claimed that Trinity had in the past exterminated its tenants in Kerry and Donegal and battened on the life-blood of the nation.

'I cannot believe,' he said, 'for it is impossible to believe, that Miss Harrison or Dunbar would serve Ireland as I would like to see Ireland served, as I believe Ireland deserves to be served. Her past has not been an Irish past and I very much doubt that her future will be an Irish future. Dr McBride has told us that Trinity College has produced some of the greatest Irishmen. True, and heaven has produced some of the greatest devils in hell. [Hear, hear.]'[12]

Councillor Higgins contended that the letter from the department was misleading. 'The word "recommend",' he said, 'would lead one to believe that we would have some say in the matter but in the next line they say they will compel us to appoint her.'[13]

The vote on Dr McBride's amendment to support Miss Dunbar Harrison was defeated by a vote of ten against and two for. Dean

D'Alton's motion was then carried by the same margin of ten for and two against. Both votes saw Rev. Jackson and Dr McBride in the minority.

Chapter 2

'Toleration would be a weakness, if not a crime'

Within days the debate had spread from the local to the national stage. On 3 December 1930 *The Irish Times* devoted a strong lead editorial to the issue.

> Our recognition of the Free State government's failings has not blinded us to its virtues. Protestants have not been penalised for their religion; in the allotment of the state's honours and prizes no discrimination has been made against them. We think that insistence on the Irish language as a test of fitness for the public services is an economic and educational folly; but it carries no taint of sectarianism, since it is imposed impartially on citizens of every creed.
>
> The establishment of the Appointments Commission abolished at one stroke an Augean stable of intrigue and jobbery. To-day a candidate for municipal office must have the commissioners' recommendation, and they have the power and the will to deal firmly with revolt.
>
> On Monday, for the second time, the [Mayo] library committee refused to ratify the commissioners' choice. Its first objection – Miss Dunbar's inadequate knowledge of Irish – failed, because all successful candidates for such appointments are entitled to opportunities for further study; the second, and more important, objection was revealed at Monday's meeting.
>
> Ten members of the committee, as against two, have declared that Protestantism, and a Dublin University degree are absolute disqualifications for public office in County Mayo. Protestantism, according to these leaders of western opinion, is an anti-national creed and Trinity College is an anti-national institution.
>
> In its refusal to appoint Miss Dunbar the library committee has defied a specific instruction from the Local Government Department. Of course, the matter can have only one end. On many occasions – especially where medical offices are concerned – local bodies, desiring their local favourites, have rejected the commissioners' recommendations. Always the commissioners have insisted on their own choice

and always they have carried the day. They are the mouthpiece of the Local Government Department, which has effective ways and means to impose its will on municipal bodies. So it must be in this case.

The government will put Miss Dunbar in office as county librarian of Mayo, and will furnish her with all necessary safeguards against local bigotry or prejudice. We believe that such action will have a beneficent influence throughout the whole country. Educated Roman Catholics will rejoice that a mainly Roman Catholic government has been so loyal to the letter and spirit of its pledges.

The wholesome significance of this affair will not be ignored in Northern Ireland. Within the Free State, Protestant minorities will feel that a certain anxiety has been lifted from their minds ... Next week the electors of County Dublin will have an opportunity to weaken Mr Cosgrave's authority and prestige. They will be astonishingly foolish if they take advantage of it ...[1]

The Irish Times was referring to an upcoming by-election in South County Dublin.

Next week's election will be a very different matter; it will be a contest between order and anarchy, between a tried system of government and a call to the maddest and most ruinous sort of political adventure. The Fianna Fáil Party, although its present speeches try to obscure the fact, is wholly impenitent. If it takes charge of the Free State's affairs, it will repudiate the Anglo-Irish Treaty, will undo all the solid work of the last eight years, and will kick the country's best customer [England] – indeed, her only customer – out of doors.

A Fianna Fáil victory in County Dublin would be a grave misfortune, since it would hearten all the forces of chaos for a frontal attack at next year's general election. We hope that, for the country's sake and their own sake, the ex-unionists of County Dublin will do their best to secure the return of Mr T.A. Finlay, K.C., who not only represents the cause of order and progress, but has personal claims to be a worthy successor of the late Major Cooper.

The case of the Mayo library committee reminds minorities in County Dublin and elsewhere that, though they may have some complaints against Mr Cosgrave's government, they have deep obligations to it.

The Irish Times was clearly not mincing its words when it came to this issue, though perhaps its blatant support of the Cumann na nGaedheal government with regard to the by-election was bound to raise the hackles of Fianna Fáil.

In its 5 December issue, *The Church of Ireland Gazette* ran an editorial which echoed that of *The Irish Times* though its tone was more measured. *The Gazette* argued that 'the action of the Mayo library committee … must inevitably increase the apprehensions which are felt by many as to the treatment which Protestants are likely to receive if certain elements in the Free State get their way.' The paper went on to absolve the Cumann na nGaedheal Party of any culpability in the matter.

> The government is in no way to blame … the particular matter may turn out to be a storm in a teacup. The disquieting feature is the reasons given for the opposition. The first was that the candidate was not well acquainted with Irish; that has now been abandoned. The main objections are that she is a Protestant and was educated at Trinity College and therefore is unfitted for a responsible post in an Irish and Roman Catholic county like Mayo.
>
> These objections were made frankly and openly by a dean and other leading priests in a meeting presided over by the Roman Catholic bishop of Killala. We cannot help asking whether they are a spokesman of a definite policy on the part of their church.
>
> We know, of course, that certain Roman Catholic papers have now for some years been urging the exclusion of Protestants from public positions of all kinds. It gives rise to great apprehension.[2]

However, the Mayo clergy were not resting on their achievements. Not content with winning the library committee's vote, Archdeacon Fallon and Dean D'Alton set about winning over public opinion. They showed no reluctance in taking their argument to the country. The letters pages of the newspapers, both local and national, were transformed into a battleground.

'Chamberlain is a very un-Irish name …'

Archdeacon Fallon was particularly active. He defended his views in a letter which *The Irish Times* captioned 'The Unsuitable Protestant'. Canon Chamberlain of Dún Laoghaire echoed the fears expressed in *The Irish Times* editorial. 'We have a signal vindication,' he said, 'of the feeling of nervous apprehension on the part of Protestants that in the Free State they would be penalised because of their religion.' He received the following reply:

> Sir, I have just read in your issue of yesterday Canon Chamberlain's comments on the proceedings of Mayo library committee at their last meeting. By the way, Chamberlain is a very un-Irish name, and possibly he does not understand our Irish 'cussedness'. As I am a member of the committee, and was present on the occasion and voted against the appointment of Miss Dunbar, I would like your readers to hear our side.
>
> I am in favour of religious tolerance. The courteous and efficient head manager of our local bacon factory is not a Catholic, and although 99% of those who transact business with him are Catholics there is always harmony and goodwill. There are Protestant doctors and solicitors in Mayo who live in peace in their community and are respected in their respective professions.
>
> I admit that toleration in general is desirable, but when Catholic fundamental principles are invaded, toleration would be a weakness, if not a crime. Miss Dunbar, I have reason to understand, is a very cultured lady, but, with all her accomplishments I maintain that as a Protestant she is absolutely unsuited for the position of librarian in the 99% Catholic population of the County Mayo … Our librarian has [in practice] the selection and the distribution of the books throughout the county. Would a Catholic librarian be appointed for a community 99% Protestant?
>
> … The Appointments Commission and the responsible minister were guilty of a grave error of judgement in recommending a Protestant for this position. It is not the first time they have ignored the local circumstances and sentiments of the people and I will be very surprised if the people will submit to this dictation much longer.[3]

Canon Chamberlain replied that, despite his Huguenot name, he fully understood Archdeacon Fallon's position though he still dissented from it. 'It is perfectly clear,' he said, 'that, if the position he has taken up be admitted, it will effectively close the door of every public library in the Free State to Protestants.'

'The conscientious bigot'

Over the following weeks the letters pages of the local and national papers became a forum for the debate. Some determined opposition emerged. Dr T. Hennessy, a medical secretary of South Frederick Street, Dublin, wrote:

> The action of the Mayo library committee in refusing to appoint Miss Dunbar to take charge of the local library because she is a Protestant and graduate of Dublin University has attracted a good deal of notice outside Ireland. Catholics who earn their livelihood in Protestant Britain are becoming anxious, as they fear retaliation. In fact, I am informed that in Liverpool and other centres reprisals have been advocated and that they should be extended to all Irish Catholic workers.
>
> Although such cases as in Mayo are few, yet they are sufficient to stimulate the 'conscientious bigot' who can only see red where Catholics are concerned. More than 80 per cent of the graduates (including those holding degrees in agriculture), of the National University have to seek a living in Protestant England and in the Protestant dominions.
>
> In the circumstances we, who live in ease and comfort in this country, should show some consideration, without sacrifice of principle, for our co-religionists who make a living in Protestant countries, and not to make such headlines as 'Where Rome Rules' for the Ku Klux Klan in America and elsewhere.
>
> Moreover, in the present instance, with such an influential, enlightened and religiously authoritative body as the Mayo library committee, if it functions conscientiously, there should be no fear from the librarian, whether he or she may be a Protestant or a capricious Catholic.[4]

If this was an appeal to national self-interest, Dean D'Alton was having none of it. Within days he was back in print in the *Irish Independent* in response to Dr Hennessy's letter outlining the potential international ramifications of the dispute.

'The "Castle Cawtholic"'

'Catholic doctors in England,' Dean D'Alton wrote, 'who do their work, have little to fear from honest Protestants, and can ignore the threats of an isolated bigot, who has not much influence in modern England. He would surely be an unreasoning bigot who expected that for such a position as librarian, and in a county almost wholly Catholic, no Catholic need apply, and this is what has happened in Mayo. In the old days every decent Irishman despised the "Castle Cawtholic". Well sir, the Castle is gone but the Cawtholic is with us still.'[5]

Dr Hennessy proved undaunted by such accusations. 'Dean D'Alton,' he countered, 'suggests I am a survivor of the despised Castle Cawtholic and apparently considers that studied retort a hushing and finishing argument. In this respect the Dean seems to overlook the little factor that not a few of his "decent" Irishmen who so loftily despised the Castle Cawtholic owed their affected sturdiness to the fact that they were green with jealousy of what they looked upon as the glittering social success of the Cawtholic.'[6]

'The Irish Times and the baser kind of Protestants'

Five days later Dean D'Alton replied. 'I am quite ready to admit,' he said, 'that the doctor is of ancient descent, and indeed, he may be, for all I know, a direct descendant of Fionn MacCumhaill … *The Irish Times* and the baser kind of Protestants have sought to brand the library committee as unwilling to allow any Protestant to be appointed to any position in Mayo. This is certainly not the case, and if the post to be filled were that of commercial instructress, or something similar, there would have been no opposition. The position of librarian, however, stands on a different footing, especially in an almost exclusively Catholic county. Much of the ordinary man's knowledge is acquired after leaving school, and from books, perhaps borrowed from a public library. In selecting these books he could get no assistance from Miss Dunbar, except, perhaps what might be harmful, and this through no fault of her own, but because of her education and outlook, which could not be expected to be national or Catholic.'[7]

'Biting on granite'

Dean D'Alton had his share of supporters on the letters pages. Thomas Concannon of Dorset Street, Dublin, was of the opinion that when the Local Appointments Commissioners came up against such men as Dean D'Alton they were 'biting on granite'.[8]

Other scribes joined in the debate with Dr Hennessy. Mr Concannon was of the opinion that Dr Hennessy was 'windy'. His letter was 'so well written, even for a doctor, that one instinctively asks – who is backing him?' He then went on to suggest an answer to his own question. 'Perhaps Dr Hennessy will be invited to drink the toast to the "Pious, Glorious and Immortal Memory of King Billy", who saved us from popes and popery. Contrary to what Dr Hennessy says, and speaking with intimate knowledge of the subject, I reiterate that Catholics – I refer more particularly to Irish Catholics – do not get, and they consider it futile to seek, higher official positions in Protestant countries. Let Dr Hennessy produce his facts and avoid generalities. It is not deniable that Catholics do occasionally pick up minor official positions, not much sought for, where the emoluments just about cover the expenses. I see Dr Hennessy is engaged in the export business. If we continue to export our brains (assuming that doctors have brains) and likewise our capital, we shall certainly progress.'[9]

Dr Hennessy's correspondence developed into a number of long-running feuds in which he gave as good as he got. Though he was fighting a lonely battle, he was not without his supporters. The Labour Party newspaper, *The Watchword*, gave him a special commendation. 'And when the honours are being distributed,' it wrote, 'let us not forget Dr Hennessy, who, in spite of some lapses, conducted a vigorous case against big odds in the press.'[10]

By 19 December the *Irish Independent* declared that they had received enough correspondence. The letters editor announced, 'We regret that we cannot allow this controversy to continue indefinitely.' However, despite declaring the correspondence closed, the *Irish Independent* continued to receive and publish numerous letters on the developing crisis.

'The hydra-headed monster of intolerance'

On 6 December 1930 *The Connaught Telegraph* published an editorial which endeavoured to bring a voice of moderation to an increasingly heated dispute. 'It would be extremely regrettable,' it wrote, 'to have the hydra-headed monster of intolerance showing its ugly form in what is essentially a business matter, but the librarianship is not like any ordinary appointment. In fact it is more in the nature of a teachership, or rather a literary instructor of the people, the most important function of which would be to select reading matter suitable to the national and Catholic needs of the people.'[11]

The editorial went on to suggest a possible compromise by placing Miss Dunbar Harrison in some other county. 'Unless this view is taken ... bitterness and a very bad taste will remain, and our library will cease to exist after the expiration of the current financial year.' This argument was impressively moderate compared to the opinions quoted in the same newspaper the following week regarding the influence of a librarian:

A librarian wields large power. He inevitably impresses his private tastes on the selection of books that he handles. His advice is sought by ill-read persons who wish to enlarge their knowledge. If he is inspired by the right ideals, he will encourage the reading of appropriate books. If he is foreign in his ideals, his library will diffuse a foreign influence. If he is not a Catholic, his standards will be different from ours ...

We are not a bigoted people. We accord to Protestants a prosperity that is immeasurably beyond their proportionate share of the country's fortunes, and we do not grudge them their shops, factories and warehouses. They have no cause for complaint. We say, however, that they have no right to occupy places in which they can propagate their doctrines among our people. We will buy our books from a Protestant; we will bank with a Protestant; but we will not let him teach our children … We will not willingly see him furnish the bulk of any Catholic reading matter in books or newspapers. We will not let him undo our censorship and spread in our country the propaganda of foreign vices. In brief, we must control our own system of education and culture. No decent Protestant challenges this reasonable claim.[12]

If this was the local attitude, conflict with the central government was inevitable.

Chapter 3

'Cesspools of infamy'

While the controversy raged in the letters pages of the newspapers, other political developments were unfolding. At the 6 December meeting of Mayo County Council the councillors approved the findings of the library committee and decided to employ legal counsel to oppose any action the minister might see fit to take to enforce the recommendation of the Local Appointments Commission. On the advice of the county secretary, M.J. Egan, the legal deliberations of the councillors were held in private. As *The Connaught Telegraph* put it, 'There was some dissent when the reporters were asked to leave.' However, undeterred by this journalistic setback, *The Connaught Telegraph* went on to give a detailed account of what had happened in the private session: 'The secretary read senior counsel's opinion, and warned the council as to their liability for costs and expenses in the event of the Department of Local Government taking "mandamus proceedings".'[1]

The fundamental question that the councillors had to ask themselves was whether or not they were acting legally? Or at the very least, on a more practical level, if it came to it, could they defend themselves in court?

Local administration was no different from any other arm of government; it acted subject to judicial review. As historian Desmond Roche puts it, 'A local authority must be able to adduce legal authority for its actions. If a local authority purports to do something in exercise of its powers but is acting beyond these powers it is said to be acting *ultra vires* and can be restrained by the High Court. On the other hand, if it fails to carry out a duty imposed by law, the court may direct it to perform the duty.'[2]

The High Court could find against the council and issue a prerogative order of mandamus. So, in essence the Department of Local Government was threatening to take the council to court so as to compel it to appoint Miss Dunbar Harrison. In this case there was the added hazard that the government had let it be known that they would hold the councillors personally liable for any costs incurred if the courts found against them.

At the end of the legal arguments the press was recalled. The public session began with Richard Walsh, the Fianna Fáil TD for Mayo South, declaring that his party would not stand for the turning down of Miss Dunbar Harrison on sectarian grounds. He did not object to Miss Dunbar Harrison on the grounds of her religion or the educational establishment from which she had graduated, while not disagreeing with the resolution of the library committee, he totally disagreed with the discussion that had taken place in reference to sectarian bias. P.J. Ruttledge, a Fianna Fáil TD for Mayo North, endorsed his party colleague's position.

Councillor Munnelly alleged that 'if Miss Dunbar was not a relative of one of the cabinet ministers she would not be forced upon us.'[3]

Councillor John Morahan of Fianna Fáil made the point that he was deviating from his own party's line. He announced that he would vote against Miss Dunbar Harrison on the grounds of religion even at the risk of being expelled from Fianna Fáil, as his duty as an Irishman and a Catholic took precedence over his membership of a political party.[4] He went on to argue that 'the weaker they thought we were in the South, the worse they would treat the Catholics in the North,' and his view was that 'they should be given tit for tat … The Catholics of the Free State should make no apology for their religion, or be deluded by any humbug about slavish tolerance having any effect in the North.'

'Tales of a council chamber'

Councillor Martin O'Donnell, a national-school teacher from Kilmeena, Westport, subsequently wrote to *The Connaught Telegraph*. 'The press, wisely or otherwise,' he said, 'was excluded from the earlier portion of the discussion, and consequently some interesting opinions, which may, some other day, come to light in "Tales of a Council Chamber" are for the present withheld from the public. I had a resolution on the matter, but, in deference to unity – happy word – withdrew it, and what appeared to me a milk-and-water attitude was taken up, wholly unworthy of the matter in dispute and unworthy of the occasion. Accepting the situation as the lesser of two evils, I refrained from saying a word in the discussion that afterwards followed.'

'The rack and the gibbet'

He then went on to express a few of the thoughts he would have said at the meeting given half a chance. 'Even if she were qualified,' he said, 'and had qualifications to spare, the unsavoury history of the past would have made her appointment most undesirable and most unsuitable and would be looked upon as a menace by many fathers and mothers of Mayo whose children are catered for from the library.

'… Trinity College, an Elizabethan institution, founded and maintained as an English outpost in Ireland, to uphold English power, English customs, English culture, and English religion … And as with Trinity, its aims and objectives, so has the whole course of English rule been directed. Time and circumstances guided the means employed. Sometimes the methods employed were brutal, sometimes peaceful; but whether it was the rack and the gibbet of Penal days, or the shooting down of innocent people at Bachelor's Walk in our own day, or the soup-kitchens of Plunkett, or the meal-tubs of the Rev. Nangle, the object was always the same – the destruction of the Irish nation, the perversion of its people.'[5]

This was a lot of guilt to lay at the feet of one young librarian.

'What a tyranny we have in our midst!' he continued. 'Was it for this our fathers struggled? And was it for this our boys fought and died? To overthrow a foreign tyranny, only to be followed by a domestic one. Substitution of tyrannies is not the definition of Freedom ... with voice and vote I'll continue to resist, and should the government by their action succeed in killing our library scheme, with regret I'll follow its hearse and hope and pray for a speedy retribution.'[6]

Such was the hostility generated by the issue that for a while it was rumoured locally that 'Miss Dunbar had withdrawn from the position, but no official confirmation could be obtained.'[7] This speculation turned out to be unfounded but it is typical of the fevered atmosphere that prevailed at the time. Given the level of controversy stirred up, it would have been little wonder if Miss Dunbar Harrison had thought better of the whole endeavour. But in December 1930 such jobs were not that easy to come by, in Ireland or elsewhere.

Perhaps the government had hoped that the mere threat of legal action would encourage Mayo's councillors to change their minds. Instead both sides had, if anything, become even more entrenched in their relative positions. Now that the council had refused to back down the ball was back in the minister's court.

'The minister's new move'

On 10 December the *Irish Independent* reported on the 'minister's new move'. General Richard Mulcahy had ordered 'a sworn inquiry to be held by Mr J. McLysaght [*sic*], inspector, at Castlebar on 17 December, into the discharge of their duties by the Mayo County Council, following their refusal to appoint Miss Letitia Dunbar as librarian for County Mayo.'[8]

The *Irish Independent's* political correspondent was also told that the minister had arrived at his decision after receiving the minutes of the County Council meeting and that he had the full support of the cabinet. The very fact that the spin doctors of their day chose to leak this information to the papers shows the pressure that Cumann na nGaedheal felt they were under. As ever there were rumours of splits within the party. Given the fact that their most senior TD in Mayo, Michael Davis, was known to be unhappy about the developing situation, this was unsurprising. *The Irish Times* confidently stated that the decision to hold an inquiry was a change of tactics by the government and that initially they had intended on 'proceeding against the council by way of "mandamus" to enforce the appointment.'[9] One can only assume that the government decided against this action based on legal advice that they might not be on strong enough grounds to win the case. And, even if their view prevailed, they would only succeed in making martyrs of the councillors in their home county.

The Irish Times went on to predict, 'If the inspector finds that the council has neglected to carry out its statutory functions, the sequel may be the suppression of the council and the handing over of its duties to a paid commissioner.'[10]

It is debatable whether threatening the council with abolition and replacement by a commissioner was politically any more acceptable than taking it to court and personally pursuing the councillors for damages. The most likely explanation for this slight change of tack is that the government decided that this was a simpler course to follow, one over which they would have more control.

The decision to hold a sworn inquiry was conveyed by telegram to the county secretary in Castlebar. The *Irish Independent* echoed the message in *The Irish Times*. 'Western deputies in Leinster House … were now asking whether the minister's step might mean the abolition of the County Council and the appointment of a commissioner.'[11] There is little doubt that this was the message the government wanted to get across, that they were in earnest and that the threat to the existence of the council was serious. The threat of dissolution, rather like being sentenced to be hanged, was designed to focus the minds of the county councillors.

As time went on the rumours grew even wilder. The *Irish Independent* repeated Councillor Munnelly's allegation that Miss Dunbar Harrison 'was a near relative of one of the chief ministers of the state.'[12] It is believed that the minister referred to was the Minister for Finance, Ernest Blythe, who was the only Protestant in the cabinet, thus emphasising the sectarian undercurrent that ran through all of the antipathy shown towards Miss Dunbar Harrison.

By this stage the dispute was creating so much turmoil that President Cosgrave decided it was time for him to step into the fray. On 11 December he made a short and carefully worded statement to the Dáil: 'The qualifications prescribed as essential for the post of county librarian,' he said, 'were a good general education and training in or experience of library work. A diploma in library training and practical experience in office organisation were stated to be desirable but not essential. A substantial preference was to be given to qualified candidates with a competent knowledge of Irish. If no such candidate were available for Mayo, the successful candidate would be required to comply with the terms of the Local Offices and Employments (Gaeltacht) Order 1928.'[13]

This order enabled successful candidates who did not have Irish to be given three years in which to learn the language.

'There were five posts to be filled,' President Cosgrave continued. 'The selection board having interviewed all the candidates reported that only five were fully qualified according to the terms of the advertisement. Two of these had a competent knowledge of Irish; the remaining three had some slight knowledge of the language. Preference having been given, as prescribed, to the two candidates who had a competent knowledge of Irish, the five candidates were placed in order of merit and a choice of the five posts was given to the candidates according to their places. The recommendation of Miss Dunbar for the appointment in Mayo resulted from these arrangements.'

President Cosgrave had detailed briefing papers with background knowledge that he did not divulge in the Dáil chamber at the time. The five county librarian vacancies to which he referred were located in Carlow, Cavan, Leitrim, Meath and Mayo.

'Miss Dunbar,' President Cosgrave continued, 'had attended a course of library training in the National University, and her library experience was obtained during a training period of one and a quarter years in the libraries of County Dublin and Rathmines. In constituting boards of selection to interview and report upon the merits of candidates for this, as well as other classes of local appointments, the Local Appointments Commissioners take care to ensure that the boards include persons possessing qualifications and experience allied to the post under consideration. In the normal course I do not know, nor does the minister know, the names of the persons who have acted on a selection board. But I called for that information in this case, and am in a position to state that the board consisted of a university professor and three librarians of much experience. As a board for the purposes of the appointments in question I am satisfied that this was a thoroughly competent one.'

In reply to a question regarding allegations of favouritism, President Cosgrave added, 'I have seen such suggestions in the press reports of speeches made at meetings in Mayo. There is no foundation whatever for these suggestions. The lady in question is not a relation of any minister – even if she were, I should not regard that as a proper ground for rendering her ineligible – but, as it happens, she is not. In regard to the allegations of religious prejudice, I may say that the Local Appointments Commissioners are not in a position to say what the religion of any particular member of a selection board may be. Selection boards are not chosen on that basis. It happens that I am personally aware that every member of this particular board was a Catholic.'[14]

It was perhaps indicative of the pressure the government felt it was under on the religious aspect of the appointment, that Cosgrave ended this carefully drafted statement with a reference to the Catholic make-up of the interview board. Not only that, a government source also let it be known to an *Irish Independent* reporter that the four other successful candidates were all Catholics.[15]

The language question was treated very much as a side issue. President Cosgrave hardly mentioned it at all in his statement. While there were some references to language, the religious aspect dominated public debate. The main opposition party, for instance, while making political capital in Mayo, also felt it had to tread carefully with regard to the sectarian facet of the dispute and the way it had come to dominate the debate. In its 13 December issue *The Nation*, Fianna Fáil's weekly newspaper, dealt directly with the language issue in a lead editorial entitled 'Miss Dunbar's Case'.

> We are glad that the two Fianna Fáil TDs [P.J. Ruttledge and Dick Walsh] who are members of Mayo County Council made the republi-can position clear with regard to public appointments in this country. The Irish people are made up of men and women of different religious beliefs and for the majority to insist upon appointments for men and women of their faith only is unjust and anti-national.
>
> There must be only one test for the public service, ability to perform the work, and that can only be discovered and recognised through com-petitive examination or some similar method by which the best wins.
>
> In Miss Dunbar's case there was obviously the fatal flaw that for a Gaeltacht appointment she had no knowledge of Irish. Our readers know how we have opposed appointments like this irrespective of the religious belief of the appointee.
>
> Miss Dunbar has not this essential qualification for an Irish-speak-ing county and therefore we believe she is not qualified to fill the posi-tion. But to declare her unfitted by religion or by the fact that she holds a Trinity degree is to re-create under the cloak of Catholicism the spirit of ascendancy which cursed this nation for 300 bitter years.[16]

However, this position was too subtle for some. The *Irish Independent* seemed confused by it. 'The Fianna Fáil Party,' it wrote, 'is apparently at one with the government in this matter. The Fianna Fáil members of Mayo County Council spoke in favour of Miss Dunbar's appointment and the weekly organ of that party, published in Dublin [*The Nation*], leaves its readers under no misapprehension as to its attitude.'[17]

This was a widely inaccurate representation of Fianna Fáil's position as Seán Ó Muineacháin, editor of *The Nation*, was quick to point out in a letter to the *Irish Independent* the following day.

The other main opposition party took a different line. *The Watchword*, the official organ of the Irish Trade Union Conference and the Irish Labour Party, gave qualified praise to William T. Cosgrave. 'Whatever may be our opposition to President Cosgrave's general policy,' it wrote, 'we have never denied his moral as well as his personal courage. And that rare quality was seen to good effect in the statement on the Mayo affair made by him in the Dáil before the adjournment. His statement was as good in form as it was in tone and it will commend itself to every citizen who refuses to make a candidate's religious – or for that matter political – faith an obligatory qualification for local or national office.'[18]

T.J. O'Connell, the leader of the Labour Party, failed to come out with as clear a statement on the affair, constrained perhaps by his own local role. He was a TD for Mayo South and was aware of how unpopular the proposed appointment of Miss Dunbar Harrison was with his electorate.

On 13 December, *The Connaught Telegraph* revisited the language question. 'Touching the linguistic aspect of the Mayo case, this is not negligible,' it wrote ' … the Irish language is the symbol of the culture of this ancient nation. People of the younger generation enjoy abundant means to familiarise themselves with Irish. Those who neglect to do it show that they do not respect the national culture – or, in a word, that they are disloyal. If persons of foreign antecedents wish to be recognised as good Irish citizens, they ought to show themselves interested in the Irish culture and Irish ideals.'[19]

By this argument, lack of knowledge of Irish was at the very least anti-national and was indeed verging on treasonable. There was a certain irony in the fact that the minister, General Richard Mulcahy, who was now defending the appointment of Miss Dunbar Harrison, was the very same minister who had been entrusted with promoting the Irish language in his role as chairman of the Gaeltacht Commission.

'The respectable skirts of nationalism'

On the other hand, many politicians, particularly those at local level, took a more straightforward approach. The ultra-conservative monthly periodical *The Catholic Mind* reserved special praise for Councillor John Morahan. Councillor Morahan had announced that he was prepared to risk expulsion from Fianna Fáil by voting against Miss Dunbar Harrison's appointment on the grounds of her Protestantism. *The Catholic Mind* wrote, 'He spurned tactics … he realised right from the beginning that Catholicity should not be smuggled in anywhere under even the respectable skirts of nationalism.'[20]

Not all local politicians were as supportive of the actions of the library committee. Some doubted their motives, questioning the sincerity of their support of the native language. Ballina Urban District Council had no direct connection with the library service administered by the County Council, yet its members took it upon themselves to debate a resolution welcoming the action of the library committee. In the process they also shed some light on the attitude of some members of the library committee towards the Irish language. Chairman McGrath voiced his opinion. 'Certainly, if ever I welcomed an action in public life,' he said, 'I welcome that. They should have Irish, the chief thing in every advertisement, but a funny thing is the stand taken by some of the committee who previously struck out against Irish … I am very glad they are converts to the Irish stand.'[21]

Councillor Carroll disagreed. He was critical of the original decision to reject Miss Dunbar Harrison. 'Reading the report of the library committee,' he said, 'it makes one sick to read some of the speeches delivered at the meeting by dignitaries of the church and laymen who don't care a *thráneen* [a straw] for the Irish language. It is simply an attack on this lady because she is a graduate of Trinity.'[22]

He went on to remind his fellow councillors 'of the fact that at one meeting of the Technical Committee, Canon Hegarty described the Irish classes in the Gaeltacht as cesspools of infamy, or words to that effect, and that was one of the gentlemen who spoke at considerable length against the appointment of the gifted graduate of Trinity College. And then you talk about imperialism emanating from Trinity College. We are up to our eyes in imperialism. We were never more sunk in it … if you put this to a vote you will be beaten.'

'There is no necessity for a vote,' interjected Chairman McGrath.

'One of the gentlemen who spoke in Castlebar never lifted his finger in the cause of the Irish language,' continued Mr Carroll.

'The motion does not come from that crowd in Castlebar. It is our own opinion, and what is expressed in the resolution is the view of the council. The resolution is passed,' replied the Chairman.[23]

Chapter 4

'The slipper lickers proceed ...'

The much-trumpeted sworn inquiry held in Castlebar on 17 December proved a tame affair. In its report the *Western People* seemed somewhat disappointed. 'The inquiry into the affairs of Mayo County Council, to which the public looked forward with such interest, is over. It lasted twenty minutes, and was entirely devoid of incident, or any of that bitterness or recrimination one might have expected under the circumstances.'[1]

According to *The Connaught Telegraph*, 'No one in the town seemed to take the least interest in the proceedings and when the inquiry began the only non-officials present were Mr P. Higgins and Mr T.S. Moclair ...'[2]

Canon Hegarty from the library committee subsequently arrived at the inquiry, as did Councillors Morahan and Jordan. Mr Seán McGrath appeared as solicitor for the council. The county secretary, Mr M.J. Egan, was also in attendance.

Opening the inquest, the inspector, Mr Séamus MacLysaght stated, 'It must be well known to you all that this inquiry has been occasioned by recent developments in the county. The pivot of the inquiry hinges on the appointment of a county librarian. It would serve no useful purpose to hold a rambling inquiry ...'[3] He went on to say that, generally speaking, the Minister for Local Government was very satisfied with the administration of the council and for that reason it was all the more regrettable that the inquiry was necessary. However, there was a statutory obligation which the council could not refuse to discharge.

Mr McGrath, on behalf of the council, stated that they welcomed the fullest and most searching inquiry. They were there to facilitate the inspector.

'The County Council feel,' Mr McGrath declared, 'that they have nothing to hide, and in fact are very proud of their tradition as perhaps the one council in Ireland in the fore-front of administration.'

Mr McGrath asked the inspector to listen to evidence about the general state of affairs in the county, but the inspector retorted that Mr Egan could give it to the press. Councillor Morahan intervened at this stage, insisting that the evidence be read to the inquiry.[4]

The county secretary then read a prepared statement of evidence as regards the financial health of the council and its activities in such areas as roads, education and the Irish language.

'Their motto and slogan,' Mr Egan declared, 'was "Economy and Efficiency".'

At the conclusion of the evidence, the inspector thanked Mr McGrath for the manner in which he had helped him.

'Mugs and thugs'

The *Mayo News* worked itself up into a fine lather of indignation over the inquiry.

> The government that has decided to dissolve the County Council is composed of some sixty persons of vapid intellect and atrophied intelligence. These persons are kept together by a lively sense of favours to come and with the cohesion of the weak witted, present a feather bag face to all attacks.
>
> With the fifty odd mugs and thugs who compose this group of compressed selfishness, we are not particularly concerned. But it is quite refreshing to find our local ciphers looking at themselves. The government of which the Cumann na nGaedheal deputies form part say 'You county councillors are either rogues or fools; we must suppress you because you are also bigots,' and the three TDs say, 'We are all rogues or fools. Suppress us because we are bigots ...'
>
> It would be quite in accordance with the facts if the government deputies endorsed the opinion of their own cabinet that they are weak witted or dishonest or both, but really they should draw the line before giving the opinion of self-confessed morons that the priests and people of Mayo are in the same class when they make the

plea 'We are humble liars, Sir', the 'we' should not include the whole population ...

It would be ungentlemanly, rude, nay, it would even appear bigoted if Mayo representatives should protest against being kicked into the gutter with a lying label on their necks for a more subservient implement than the council succeeded in being. BUT THE COUNCIL PROTESTS AND THE SLIPPER LICKERS PROCEED [Capitals, *Mayo News's* own].

'From Irish pigs to Irish policemen'

And meanwhile all the 'broad-minded' people were condemning the library committee. Gentlemen who can read but don't were showing that they were not like the common ruck of papists. Some of them had read three or four books even. And from the height of their literary attainments, sneered at the bigotry of the unlettered, and after these litterateurs came the battalion of economists. They as a rule, boasted that they had never read any book but assured the world that England would retaliate. England would boycott everything from Irish pigs to Irish policemen. For the first time since 1916 we had a clear division, verminous slipper lickers on one side and the people who stand upon their feet on the other.[5]

The *Mayo News* revealed some information from an obviously well-connected source. 'On Thursday morning [18 December],' it wrote, 'it was learned in Castlebar that the government's legal advisers had informed the cabinet that they had no legal status in their attempt to get a mandamus against the council ...' The government was now 'taking steps to dissolve the council.'[6]

The Minister for Local Government, Richard Mulcahy, was considered one of the 'hard men' of his party. He had been very close to Michael Collins and had delivered the eulogy at his funeral. He had been Minister for Defence in the previous Dáil but had been forced to resign for his role in the Army Mutiny in 1924. He later made his political comeback as Minister for Local Government and Public Health.

Fianna Fáil tended to avoid direct attacks on President Cosgrave, preferring to concentrate their criticisms on Richard Mulcahy. As Minister for Local Government he was the main target of the political opposition to Miss Dunbar Harrison's appointment. However, Edward P. McCarron, secretary of the department, also became embroiled in the dispute. Mr McCarron was a career civil servant who had worked for the British administration in Ireland pre-1921 as a local government auditor, class 1, and had continued his career in the Free State in the Department of Local Government. In 1922 his appointment to a senior post in the Free State civil service had been controversial. The following excerpt from the Dáil gives a flavour of the proceedings:

> Deputy Joseph McDonagh asked the Minister for Local Government, 'Is it a fact that Mr McCarron offered his services to the British military in Drogheda in Easter week?'
>
> To which the Minister for Local Government replied, 'I cannot say whether it is a fact. I was not in Drogheda in Easter week.'[7]

This was hardly a ringing endorsement for Mr McCarron. He was greatly distrusted by many local authorities as the Cosgrave government strived to re-assert central control over some of the wayward county councils. Having worked for the British administration in Ireland, Mr McCarron was in many ways a convenient whipping boy; he was seen as a remnant of colonial rule and was cordially detested, especially by Fianna Fáil and Sinn Féin. Another rumour that was circulated about him was that he had tried to enlist in the British army during the First World War.[8]

The *Mayo News* devoted an impressive amount of venom to Mr McCarron and his perceived role in the Mayo affair. 'And now we come to the hero of the piece, Mr E.P. McCarron,' it wrote. 'He is the great little council smasher of the decade. For his English masters during the late Redmondite period any council that was not sufficiently pro-British was smashed. After the 1916 War of

Independence, any council that dared to employ Irish rebels was smashed (signed E.P. McCarron). During the aftermath of the war any public body that did not hunt out those with Irish leanings got their quietus signed E.P. McCarron.

'During the Black and Tan terror the councils that were not pro-British and Tan had to go into hiding per orders signed E.P. McCarron. After the Treaty, councils that worked to bury the hatchet of civil war had their pro-Irish officials hunted, signed E.P. McCarron. What is the secret behind all this? That E.P. McCarron will serve anyone who pays his salary?'[9]

Meanwhile there was unrest in the county. The *Leitrim Observer* reported a 'protest by peasants'. 'At a meeting at Louisburgh on Sunday thousands of peasants protested against the appointment of an official lacking an adequate knowledge of the native tongue.'[10]

The report submitted to the department by Mr Séamus MacLysaght was short and to the point. Save for their action in refusing to sanction the appointment of Miss Dunbar Harrison, Mayo County Council was given a clean bill of health.

'Personal pecuniary responsibilities'

Richard Mulcahy ensured that the results of the inspector's inquiry were published in the national and regional newspapers. In a government notice, a copy of the letter to Mayo County Council signed by E.P. McCarron, secretary of the Local Government Department, was published in full. The report commenced, 'The Minister for Local Government and public health directs me to state, for the information of the Mayo County Council, that he has received the report of the local inquiry held on the 17th …' The conclusion of the report is as follows:

This evidence shows conclusively that the council acting with full knowledge refused to give effect to the appointment of Miss Dunbar, a person recommended by the Local Appointments Commissioners to fill the vacant post of county librarian for Mayo. The recommendation was made in accordance with the provisions of the Local Authorities (Officers and Employees) Act, 1926. The council, therefore, had no function in this matter other than to invite Miss Dunbar to take up duty. In refusing to do so the council has failed to give effect to a statutory duty.

... The minister for his part is advised that upon him rests the statutory duty of ensuring that due effect is given to the recommendation of the Local Appointments Commissioners. Since the inception of the act nearly 1,000 recommendations have been made by the Appointments Commissioners, and in all cases the local authority concerned has appointed the person recommended where such person was willing to accept the appointment.

... The recommendation of the Local Appointments Commissioners was made over four months ago, and the delay which has already occurred in appointing Miss Dunbar to the position to which she is legally entitled is unreasonable. Apart from that consideration, members of the council are placing themselves needlessly in the invidious position of assuming personal pecuniary responsibilities.

... In all other respects the County Council since election have administered faithfully the laws of the Oireachtas. For that reason and because, as already indicated, of the possibility that some doubt remains as to the true facts, the minister considers the council are entitled to a further opportunity of considering the matter. I am accordingly to say that a final decision will not be taken until 1 January ...[11]

Now that the government had received the anticipated report from the inspector the next move was to give Mayo County Council an opportunity to change its stance. Using the excuse of a letter written by Canon Hegarty, which called into question Miss Dunbar Harrison's eligibility on the grounds of age and experience, the department gave the Council one last opportunity to reconsider. The fact that Miss Dunbar Harrison had been born in February 1906 and was under the twenty-five-year age requirement was yet another revelation calling into question her appointment.[12]

Chairman Michael Davis refused to have anything to do with the convening of a special meeting, so the county secretary, M.J. Egan, took it upon himself to organise it. Canon Hegarty's letter seems little more than a pretext, which served to get the matter back on the agenda despite the fact that the council had already met and voted on it. The following notice was issued to each member of the County Council by M.J. Egan:

> You are hereby summoned to attend a special meeting of the Mayo County Council to be held in the Council Chamber, Courthouse, Castlebar, at the hour of one o'clock p.m., on Saturday, 27 December 1930, to consider communication from the Minister for Local Government and public health in regard to the council's refusal to appoint Miss Dunbar as county librarian, and to consider their former decision on the matter in light of the facts set out in the minister's letter.[13]

The meeting was arranged for Saturday, 27 December, just days before the government's self-declared deadline of 1 January. As the *Leitrim Observer* asked, 'Is it the olive branch?' The paper went on to declare that 'Mayo was always a model loyal body, and never flung the glove to the department until the present situation arose.'[14] It could be argued that the councillors weren't being offered much of an olive branch if at the same time they were being reminded of their 'personal pecuniary responsibilities'.

The government had let it be known, by every means possible, that they were absolutely determined to abolish the council if it did not change its mind and accept Letitia Dunbar Harrison as county librarian. Nevertheless the ball was back in the council's court and it was up to them to make the next move.

Chapter 5

'They will boycott your funeral'

It could be argued that all of the actions taken by the government during the Mayo affair were as much to defend the Local Appointments Commission as they were to protect the rights of Miss Letitia Dunbar Harrison. The Commission was a newly established body and this was the first time that a County Council had seriously questioned one of its job recommendations.

The LAC was a central agency that had been set up to provide independent assessment of recruitment to local bodies and thereby combat favouritism, nepotism and political patronage. Candidates were to be judged on their professional merits, rather than their connections. There had been a general feeling, 'amounting almost to a tradition, that local councils could not be trusted to fill jobs fairly.'[1] Canvassing and dishonesty were widely suspected. Arthur Griffith had long planned for a centralised recruitment system for both public and civil service jobs. This had been the policy of the Sinn Féin Party from which Cumann na nGaedheal had emerged.

There are many examples from the early years of the twentieth century, of local bodies selecting patently unsuitable candidates ahead of better-qualified applicants. Given the lack of central control, it comes as little surprise that canvassing and nepotism were rife. Libraries proved no exception to the opportunity for local duplicity.

One well-known case occurred in Limerick. As one library historian put it, 'It was not only in small towns that such jobbery and corruption took place. A disgraceful case of favouritism was the appointment of James McNamara as the first librarian of Limerick library.'[2] Andrew Carnegie had given the city the substantial sum of £7,000 with which to build a new library. A museum was also incorporated into the planned building. In May 1906 Limerick Corporation advertised for the joint post of museum curator and director of the library. The salary was set at £110 a year with the added perk of a residence in a house adjacent to the library. Seventeen applications were received. This was reduced to a short list of four.

It was resolved to hold a written examination to decide between the remaining contestants. Even at this early stage one of the four candidates suspected foul play. He 'did not offer himself because he believed no matter what his qualifications might be the result was a foregone conclusion.'[3]

A level of Irish 'up to the standard of the pass degree of the Royal University' was a requirement for the job. A written as well as an oral test in Irish was held for the three candidates who presented themselves. The other written papers were in Irish history and antiquities, bibliography (knowledge of books) and freehand drawing. The *Cork Examiner* stated of one candidate that he 'has to all appearance no grip of the subject. He, therefore, I take it, does not come into consideration at all.' However, that was not the way it worked out. This particular candidate, a Mr James McNamara, despite failing to qualify in written Irish, oral Irish or bibliography (in which test he received the princely sum of zero marks), was selected for the post.

The employment of James McNamara was not without opposition. He was chosen only on the casting vote of the chairman of the library committee. In the initial vote taken, Mr McNamara and Mr Thomas Stephens, who was the only candidate to qualify in all the subjects, each received twenty-eight votes.[4] Both candidates were local, but James McNamara seems to have been better connected.

Job selection in this manner became little more than a popularity contest. Local politicians, due to the fact that they themselves depended on votes, were particularly susceptible to local lobbying. The case in Limerick is perhaps only unusual in that the bias was so blatant. This was just one example of what could happen at a local level. It was widely believed that who you knew was more important than what you knew when it came to getting a job with a local council. As Jasper Wolfe, TD, put it, 'When I was a member of a public board – it is a shame for me, I suppose, to have to confess it, but we all know the facts – I, like the other members voted for the man I knew best or for the candidate whose friends I knew best, but I never voted for a relative. I did like everybody else. It was the common custom. We all held it to be our duty to vote for the candidate we knew best or whose friends we knew best.'[5] It was the intention of the Cumann na nGaedheal government to regularise such appointments by standardising the employment procedures. They did this by setting up an independent body to oversee the recruitment process.

In 1926 the Local Authorities (Officers and Employees) Act was drawn up to implement this centralised recruitment policy. One of its first steps was to establish the Local Appointments Commission which was given the power to select and recommend persons for appointment to principal posts in local authorities; the categories specified were chief executive officers and technical and professional posts. County librarian posts were among those covered by the act. Local authorities were bound to appoint the candidate recommended.

As the minister moving the bill in the Dáil, James Burke, put it: 'Charges of nepotism and corruption have occasionally been made against local authorities. We are, unfortunately, in the position where we are able to confirm those charges, and while I do not say that either corruption or nepotism is carried out on any great scale in appointments made by local authorities, at the present time, yet there is some foundation for the statement. But even if there was no foundation for such a statement, it is undoubtedly true that the best representatives of local authorities object very much to the continual canvassing that goes on with regard to appointments by local authorities, and they would be very glad, as we are glad, to be divested of all patronage with regard to these appointments.'[6]

Fianna Fáil did not take up their seats in the Dáil in 1926 so it was left to the Labour Party and the Farmers' Party to act as the opposition. They had serious reservations about the proposed legislation. While they may have felt that there was a problem, the measure proposed by Cumann na nGaedheal was seen as too drastic a curtailment of local democracy. As Deputy Pádraig Baxter pointed out, the passing of this act would result in a complete change in the procedure for making professional appointments to local authorities. 'If we pass this measure,' he said, 'the Commission will make the appointment, to be sanctioned by the minister ... the local authorities will not have one word or one voice in that.'[7]

As a possible compromise it was suggested that the Commission should pass on a short list of successful candidates in order of merit, from which the local authorities might then make their selection. Many deputies opposed the principle of the bill on the grounds that it stripped local authorities of one of its few remaining powers. Tom Johnson of the Labour Party was one of those. 'I think the minister is moving very rapidly,' he said, 'in the direction of making membership of a local authority so mean and petty an office as only to attract the meanest and pettiest minds in the country.'[8]

The Minister for Finance, Ernest Blythe, defended the proposal stating: 'People who desire appointments will, in the main, be pleased with it, because those who are defeated will be satisfied if somebody better than themselves gets the appointment, and it will be in the interests of the ratepayers. I think that we should not pay any attention to the kind of outcry that will arise from people who like to exercise patronage. There are always people who are pulling strings, and there are people who pulled strings in the past.'

'And in the minister's constituency particularly,' interjected Deputy Baxter.[9]

'An orgy of jobbery'

Minister for Justice, Kevin O'Higgins, declared, 'The fact is that up and down the country members of public bodies, members of farmers' unions, and members of other organisations have been talking of an orgy of jobbery and about appointments to the public service on grounds other than a man's capacity to perform the particular function assigned to him.' O'Higgins got to the heart of the debate, 'On this question as to who performs the formal act of appointment, if the appointment is to be automatic on the recommendation of the tribunal, does it matter in whom it lies? … The reason for prescribing in the bill that that act shall be performed by the minister is … that where a name is sent down, which is not the name that was desired by a majority of a particular local body, you are courting the position that they will refrain from making a particular appointment, and you do not want simply to court that kind of clash to secure that where the appointment is duly made, you would almost have to dissolve the local body and appoint a commissioner.'[10]

Deputy Louis D'Alton disagreed with the thrust of the bill. 'These representatives on public bodies,' he said, 'have been appointed by the people as custodians of their affairs. But they are to be told that they cannot be trusted unless they are under the direction of a mastermind that can say, "You can go so far but not further." In this matter the minister is simply putting a pitchfork before the tide. If there are boards in Ireland that do not do their duty it is for the people to get rid of their representatives on these boards.'

Deputy Gorey was of a similar opinion. 'What object have we now,' he asked, 'in calling this department the Local Government Department, or calling the minister, Minister for Local Government? It is the Department of Central Government and he is Minister for Central Government. Local authority and local jurisdiction is gone. Under the bill every vestige of what was local authority resides now with the minister. Not a single appointment can be made, not even a roadmaker or a stonebreaker can be appointed by the local authorities.'[11]

Deputy Patrick J. Egan was strongly in favour of the bill. 'Public representatives,' he said, 'are assailed from all directions in connection with these appointments. If you do not vote for the relatives of your friends on a council they will boycott your funeral.'[12]

Following a number of amendments, listing certain exceptions among middle- and lower-level posts that would be excluded from the Commission's remit, the act passed through the Dáil. Two years later, following two general elections and the assassination of Kevin O'Higgins, Fianna Fáil dropped its abstentionist policy and took its place in the Dáil as the biggest opposition party. In 1928 Eamon de Valera sponsored a private members' bill to curtail the powers of the Local Appointments Commission, 'the chief one being that where the act provides for sending down the name of one person, it shall be discretionary for local bodies to ask that instead of a single name being sent down to them for an appointment, a panel of names be sent to them.'[13]

Unsurprisingly, Cumann na nGaedheal opposed the bill. President Cosgrave was insisted that their act 'was introduced for one main purpose and that was to secure in the appointment of officials of local authorities the very best qualified persons for each post vacant … what is the purpose of sending down more than one name except to invite the local authority to appoint someone other than the best? … What about the poor man's son? What about the rights of democracy if there is not some premium for talent and capacity to fill these offices?'[14]

'The shortest cut from Knockna-Skeherooh to Mowamanahan'
Deputy Hennessy was also sceptical of the value of sending down three names. 'I have heard something about local experience,' he said. 'I do not know what that means … I believe that the interpretation

of "local man" is one who knows the shortest cut from Knockna-Skeherooh to Mowamanahan in the Knockmealdown Mountains.' During the debate that followed Richard Mulcahy stated, 'In order to clear the air I want to say that the Local Government Department, and the present executive, are not going to accept for consideration a suggestion from any public body, or from any other body, no matter who, that there should be discrimination in matters of religion in the making of appointments, either under the central government or under local authorities.'[15]

Seán Lemass alleged, 'I know men and I do not want to produce their names in this house, who were appointed as dispensary doctors by the Local Appointments Commissioners and who have not been sober since the day they were appointed.'[16]

Deputy Gorey alleged that 'whether it was the peculiar atmosphere of the Shannon mud that was responsible for it or not, I do not know, but so it was anyhow. Before the war, when money was not as plenty as it was later on, it took £750 to £800 to get a doctor elected in Limerick. Anybody who had not that amount was out of it. That was supposed to be the market price at the time.'[17]

The Fianna Fáil bill was defeated, but later in 1928, on foot of an undertaking that had been given during the debate by President Cosgrave to Deputy T.J. O'Connell of the Labour Party, a select committee of the Dáil was set up to inquire into the workings of the LAC. The committee circularised the 249 local bodies in the Free State, asking them to submit in writing any representations they wished to make. Of these, 132 chose not to reply. Of the remaining 117, a total of 7 expressed satisfaction, 23 were opposed on principle, 20 had no observations to make and 67 suggested various improvements.[18]

The committee's report was seen as generally favourable of the LAC. The act responsible for setting up the LAC was undoubtedly well intentioned but it was perhaps a flawed piece of legislation and the only surprise might have been that it was over four years before a local authority mounted a serious challenge to it.

Chapter 6

'Lapses into poetry'

The special meeting of Mayo County Council began promptly at 1 p.m. on Saturday, 27 December. Pat Higgins opened proceedings by inviting Michael J. Egan, the county secretary, to read into the minutes a number of items of correspondence from the Department of Local Government outlining the reasons for the assembly. The *Western People* reported that the discussion was, 'if not a feast of reason, a flow of soul. It was on the whole good tempered, though there was an amusing undercurrent of understanding of the members who had been "got at" since the last meeting.'[1]

The *Roscommon Herald* was of a similar opinion. 'The debate was not the conversational style of discussion usual at County Council meetings,' it wrote. 'Every speaker made quite a long speech and it was evident that few of the speeches were extempore. Most of the orators spoke from typescript and in some instances there was a reversion to the style of the days of Grattan, Burke and Sheridan … with flowery language … dramatic declamation … animated gesticulation and lapses into poetry.'[2] The *Roscommon Herald* offered one possible explanation for this type of oratory. 'Just as not many years ago the preponderance of lawyers in a certain political league earned for it the title of "The League of the Seven Attorneys" so Mayo's premier public body, after Saturday's proceedings, can be termed "The Council of the Nine Schoolmasters".'[3]

The report, examining the workings of the council, was submitted to the department by Séamus MacLysaght, as was a letter from E.P. McCarron, of the Department of Local Government, directing Mr Egan to call a meeting of the council for the purpose of giving the body the opportunity to reverse its original decision not to appoint

Miss Dunbar Harrison as county librarian. As the *Western People* put it, by appointing her the council would save itself from 'immediate relegation to oblivion.'

Mr Egan explained that he had been in touch with Michael Davis, the council chairman, in connection with the calling of the special meeting, but that Deputy Davis had refused to accept any responsibility for its summoning. He declined to attend, so Mr Egan had gone ahead and summoned it on his own responsibility as directed by the Minister for Local Government, Richard Mulcahy. Martin O'Donnell intervened, asking whether it was right and proper that the council should be asked to look into an issue on which they had already made a decision.

'According to law,' he said, 'we cannot take up the matter again for six months. On whose instructions are you going?'

'I expect I'm going on instructions from the minister,' replied Mr Egan.

To which Councillor O'Donnell responded ironically, 'That's alright then.'[4]

In the eyes of many of the observers it did not seem, in truth, that the councillors greatly minded revisiting the debate. Given the widespread interest that had been stirred up in the community at large, they welcomed the opportunity to air their views in public. First up was Pat O'Hara, an independent councillor, 'a tall, heavily built man with a big voice and assertive manner', who proposed that Miss Dunbar Harrison be appointed on the grounds that the Local Appointments Commission had been set up by the Dáil for the purpose of filling such posts.[5] Irish was not an essential requirement. As was commonplace with many other posts at the time, if in three years Miss Dunbar Harrison still did not have Irish then her appointment could be revoked.

'We are the connecting link between the ratepayers and the Dáil,' said Councillor O'Hara. 'We are here to give vent to our grievances and if we are dissolved it is only professional men and

TDs that will rule the county and perhaps it will end in revolution in a short time.'

There was laughter from the gallery to which Councillor O'Hara responded, 'There was often revolution for less. Handing over the administration of our county to a man we don't know at all. And when this gentleman comes down here it is not the appeal from the poor he will pay attention to but the appeal from the professional gentlemen or some other body. I say for the sake of this trifling matter it is better for us to have a little bit of common sense and not to dissolve the council ... The game is not worth the candle. Let us not dissolve the council and be a laughing stock for England and Ireland.'[6]

Councillor Mullarkey suggested a three-minute limit be imposed on speeches but there was no support forthcoming.

Councillor Duffy seconded Councillor O'Hara's proposal. The Local Appointments Commission had been in existence for only a few years yet it had already recommended over a thousand candidates to various positions. This was the sole case in which a recommendation had been made but not carried out. What was the point of the LAC if its recommendations were ignored? The LAC had been established by the Dáil. It was set up for a good reason.

'I consider the law that gave you the Appointments Commission was a good one because in the County Roscommon, quite convenient to where I live, a few years ago bribery was so rampant that one of the councillors had to do a term in jail,' said Duffy.

'That was not Mayo,' Chairman Higgins pointed out.

'Stick to Mayo,' a heckler shouted.

'The Castlebar way'

'I consider the taking of the appointments out of the hands of the county councils was a step in the right direction. In the present instance there were some applicants from Castlebar ...'

'Why single out Castlebar?' Councillor Moclair asked.

'They want to do this the Castlebar way,' Councillor Duffy replied, 'the same as every other.'

'There should be no invidious comparisons,' Councillor Moclair insisted.

'And as a Castlebar man,' Councillor Morahan added, 'I resent the attack on Castlebar.'[7]

The chairman intervened to restore order. He 'made a motion as if to separate the two N.T.'s [national teachers] who glared at each other, but he was out of reach.'[8]

'I am over thirty years in public administration in Mayo and I challenge Mr Duffy or any other man to say there was ever corruption in County Mayo,' he asserted, to rapturous applause from the public gallery.

'Mr Duffy is like a man sent here to irritate people,' interjected Councillor O'Donnell.

'I ask for your protection, Mr Chairman,' Councillor Duffy pleaded.

'Go on.'

In the calmer atmosphere that followed, Councillor Duffy continued, arguing that Irish was not a compulsory requirement. 'As far as her appointment and her training and her religion are concerned it is practically a matter of indifference to the county.'

'So was souperism,' commented Councillor Morahan.

'There is a library committee to select the books to be used in the county. We have also a censorship in Ireland whereby any books unreadable by Catholic people would be prevented from coming to the library. Of the books read in Ireland today 90 per cent are written by Protestants.'

'Scrap the library,' suggested a heckler.

'Some say the council should be wiped out,' shouted another.

'And damn little loss,' came a third cry.

'That may be but I will not stand for the expense of a surcharge,' said Councillor Duffy.

Having said his piece Councillor Duffy returned to his seat. Councillor Dick Walsh, a Fianna Fáil TD, rose next. He began by accusing Councillor Pat O'Hara, an independent, of hoping to gain a Cumann na nGaedheal nomination for the upcoming general election. He conceded that while Fianna Fáil had accepted the setting up of the Local Appointments Commission, they had wanted it to send the names of three successful candidates to the local authorities and they would select their preference from those three. He spoke up in favour of Councillor O'Donnell.

'How can our standing orders be set aside?' he asked. 'It shows the position we are in that we have absolutely no power here at all and though we are sent here by the people we really have no power. The minister by a stroke of his pen can tear up our standing orders and they do not matter a row of pins.[9]

'We are the first county that has thrown down the challenge to them,' Walsh asserted to cries of 'Hear, Hear' from his colleagues and the gallery, 'and that is one of the principal issues I am fighting here today, the system, this rotten system and that is what we must fight, the system that makes us go to the bother of getting elected and then tells us we don't matter a row of pins.'

'Doing away with the ratepayers' money,' came a cry from the gallery.

'Honest mistakes'

'They appointed a committee of inquiry,' Councillor Walsh continued, ' ... there is no Mayo man or member of the council here who has any need to be ashamed of the result ... I say that for all parties, regardless of what party the members represent. My experience of public bodies so far as it has gone on in this county has been that while men differed, and often had bitter differences on political questions, when it came to the affairs of the county they did their honest best ['Hear, Hear']. If mistakes were made they were honest mistakes and no one had any reason to be ashamed of what they did. I would ask the members of the council today not to stultify themselves, not to creep, not to eat dirt. The issue is knit. Let them, if they are true to the traditions of this council and this county, stand to the position they took up before the last day, and let us all bear our share of whatever is coming, and I can assure the members of this council anyhow, we will do that and stick to the decision arrived at.'[10]

Councillor Walsh sat down to cheers and applause from the gallery. 'Several members rose to speak, but the acting chairman decided to give his own views.'[11]

'Gentlemen,' Pat Higgins began, 'I thought when the question of librarianship was last before us that we had decided to cross the Rubicon, to burn our boats and to pledge ourselves never to return. I want to know what has happened in the interval to alter the situation or to change our minds. Yes, an inquiry has been held and you are given another chance of retracing your steps and doing penance for your sins, of preparing a reception for Miss Dunbar, of taking off your hats and leading her triumphantly to Mayo's capital.'[12]

Pat Higgins then recalled another episode in Mayo's history, when a similar attempt by a foreign government to impose upon the county a system of 'Godless schools and Godless colleges' had been foiled by an illustrious ecclesiastic. The 'Great McHale, the Lion of the Fold of Judah' sprang to his feet and crippled that attempt in the first hour of its existence.

'We are threatened with pains and penalties,' Councillor Higgins continued. 'What will our answer be today to all those threats? Let our answer be true and clear, let it be that Mayo County Council having taken up our position on this question, neither the brow-beating threats of General Mulcahy nor the miserable scoffing of "Castle Catholics" will drive us from that position. [Cheers] All Ireland is watching this council chamber and all Ireland expects you will stand firm. [Applause]'[13]

Councillor Bernard Joyce from Ballinrobe declared that he had been a member of the library committee that had taken the original decision and that if he had had any misgivings then, now he had none, as recent events had made him even more convinced that the resolution of the library committee was perfectly justified. He was critical of President Cosgrave's Dáil statement that Miss Dunbar Harrison had been given a choice of counties and had chosen Mayo.

'Wouldn't it be more proper,' he said, 'for the department responsible to say to the best and most qualified of these persons, "You will be sent to Mayo, you will be sent to the west – to a Gaelic county." But I am pleased to say it is a county that is a credit to Ireland, second to none in Ireland.'

Wild applause issued from the gallery.

'Wouldn't you think,' Councillor Joyce continued, 'it would be more creditable to the minister to say, "You must take up the position in Mayo? But God help us when all the others were satisfied, it is good enough for you. Go down to Mayo." Now I say that is a reflection on the dignity of the people of this county, and it is not fair to the people of this county. I don't want to say one word with regard to this lady; personally, I feel for the young lady but I object to the system of making an appointment that is unsuitable to the people all over every county as well as this one. The president also said that there were no other candidates fully qualified except the four, and that two of these only were qualified in Irish. Is that correct? How can we challenge that?'

'We do,' Councillor Morahan interjected. 'It is wrong.'

'I have been told it is wrong,' argued Councillor Joyce, 'and if it is, why should any department make a wrong statement to the people of Mayo?'

'They will have to answer to Mayo,' warned Councillor Morahan.

Councillor Joyce 'relied on documentary evidence to give his views weight.'[14] 'I think I have a little information here that proves they are wrong,' he said. 'I received a letter this morning from Monsignor D'Alton, PP, Ballinrobe, the Dean of the Archdiocese of Tuam. It is a letter he received from a young lady who made an application for the position but he told me he has not got permission from the young lady to publish her name. I will just read the letter to you to prove that the department was making statements to this council that were not true.'[15]

He then proceeded to read the text of this letter into the minutes.

'Gentlemen, that young lady was the required age, Miss Dunbar was not. She was qualified in Irish; Miss Dunbar had practically no knowledge of Irish. She has the diploma in library training and Miss Dunbar has practically no such diploma.'

He concluded, 'I have great pleasure in asking this council to stand by the resolution of the Mayo library committee submitted here on two occasions and that will put an end to this long controversy. If they want to dismiss the council let them do so.' Councillor Joyce sat down to warm applause.

Councillor O'Donnell then proposed a motion, seconded by Councillor Joyce, 'that we the members of Mayo County Council, called together by request of the Minister for Local Government to reconsider our attitude to the recommendation of the Local Appointments Commission regarding the appointment of Miss Dunbar as librarian for County Mayo, beg to point out to the minister that we have already unanimously refused to appoint or invite the young lady mentioned. This decision on our part is definite and irrevocable and we are of the opinion that no useful purpose can be served by further discussion.'

Councillor O'Donnell gave as his reasons – that Miss Dunbar Harrison had no Irish, that she was a graduate of Trinity College and as such must be imbued with West-British sentiments, and thirdly that she was not a Catholic.

'I am very sorry,' he said, 'that this question of religion has to be brought in, but I bring it in and I have nothing to apologise for or to be ashamed of. I am not a bigot; I am not hostile to her being a Protestant, but the library is an educational institution in this county and the idea of appointing a Protestant to it is, as I say, intolerable. If this county was as Protestant as it is today Catholic, I would object to a Catholic having this position, it would be most intolerable, unsuitable, regrettable and unfortunate to have a Catholic in charge.'

'Is this to go on all day?' Councillor O'Hara enquired.

'Don't mind them,' replied Councillor O'Donnell. 'They are sent here for this purpose. I say history is repeating itself. I don't want to go into it, but let it not be pushed too far. I would be very sorry that anything should occur here that would upset these good relations [between the councillors].'

'A migratory Micawber'

'What has occurred since the first meeting that would make us alter our views?' continued Councillor O'Donnell. 'We are lectured and who are the lecturers? Who are the men who tell us what we should do? The first a Presbyterian from Belfast, then a doctor from Galway who tells us he spent sixty years in England and then a kind of migratory Micawber named Mr O'Malley, plying between Athlone and London. A Presbyterian minister, probably an army doctor in England and the other tramp politician, are these the men we would apply to, to ask what would be suitable for a Mayo library?

'I hold nothing has occurred since that we need to be ashamed of. Mayo always held its own and it will hold its own now,' he asserted, to cheers and cries of 'Up Mayo!' and 'O'Donnell Abu!' from the gallery, which seemed to surprise the speaker.

'Mayo made a stand against tyranny in the past and it will stand against tyranny now,' he concluded.

Councillor Duffy complained that the chairman wasn't keeping to standing orders. 'It is all Castlebar as usual,' he said.

'Look here,' Councillor Morahan responded, 'you mention Castlebar again and I for one man will fire you outside the door.'

There were great cheers in the gallery and cries of 'Good man, Johnny.'

Councillor O'Donnell continued, 'I would appeal to the council to be unanimous for the sake of what we stand for in Mayo. I would say to those who come to lecture us, whether *The Irish Times* or the individuals, I object to Trinity College not because it is Protestant but because it is un-Irish. It is anti-Irish and anti-Catholic, if you will. Every day don't we see where it flies the flag of that other country in our eyes? Are we going to be pro-Britons and submit to them? Are we going to be browbeaten into allegiance to the Trinity way or that of *The Irish Times*?'

Councillor O'Donnell concluded by asking the council not to rescind their previous order, because if they did they would be met with nothing but contempt.

Councillor Morahan was next to speak, and he delivered a well-prepared speech:

> At our last meeting I took a stand against the appointment of a Trinity Protestant and non-Irish speaking candidate to the position of county librarian in Catholic Gaeltacht Mayo, and despite Minister Mulcahy's threat to mint a new brand of Seán na Sagart, despite the threat of abolition by a whilom tool of England, Mulcahy's professional council breaker, I stand unflinchingly where then I stood, and were I to stand in that attitude alone today, I should still cry out, 'Come one, come all, this rock shall fly from its firm base as soon as I.'[16] The kindly Celtic people of Mayo are solidly against this appointment.
>
> I challenge any Protestant professional man or trader residing in Mayo to say Mayo is bigoted. And yet while we kindly people acknowledge the right of those differing from us in religion to live among us and on us, we enshrine the principle that education is based on and lives around religion, and we are determined that our library as an education centre, serving a county of 99 per cent Catholics, shall never be placed in the charge of a Protestant.

Are we bigots? Rise up you kindly Celtic hillsides, by whose rocks our priests and people were butchered. Are we bigots? Flow on, you noble rivers of Ireland, your ripples testifying to a treachery that choked your courses with the lifeless bodies of Celtic women and children. Are we bigots? Whisper you waves that lap up our coasts, an echo of the agonising caoin [cry] that rent the air as the slave-ships and coffin-ships, loaded with their human freight, departed from kindly Celtic shores.

Take up that echo, you kindly Celtic wind and waft it to this council chamber. We are listening. We are not bigots; neither are we knaves. The story of this kindly Celtic people's suffering for their religion is written in letters of blood across the pages of our country's history. Through centuries of persecution and relentless torture, our ancestors have handed down to us the glorious heritage of the True Faith.

That treasure we zealously guard, and we are determined, come what may, and never, never again, will we allow a bigoted minority to creep into our strongholds and drench our land with kindly Celtic blood. They have razed our proudest castles, spoiled the temples of the Lord, burned to dust the sacred relics, put the people to the sword, desecrated all things holy as they soon may do again, if their power today we smite not, if today we be not men.[17]

'Poison gas to the kindly Celtic people'

I am opposed to the appointment of a product of Trinity to the position of librarian in this county. Trinity culture is not the culture of the Gael; rather is it poison gas to the kindly Celtic people. We know the history of Trinity; we are aware of what it stands for today. It is the bigoted anti-Irish outpost of England in Ireland. It is a spurious outgrowth, having no roots in Irish soil. In the past it fed like a parasite on the flesh and blood of our kindly Celtic people, and if we mean to preserve our distinctly Gaelic culture we must check the progress of the pest.

Miss Dunbar Harrison with her Trinity culture is not a fit person to place in charge of a county library as a centre of culture for Mayo. I am opposed to the appointment of Miss Dunbar Harrison to the position of county librarian in Gaeltacht Mayo on the grounds of her incompetency in the native language. Irish is the official language of the state as laid down in the Constitution. Trinity ignores the Constitution by refusing to place the official language as a compulsory subject in its curriculum.

Miss Dunbar Harrison gives Irish no place, and she now comes forward for a position in the gift of the Constitution she and her university defied. At the command of the bigoted and Freemason Press, Catholic rights are ignored. The unanimous voice of Mayo's representatives is flouted, and the minister is prepared to violate Article 8 of the Constitution. I should not be surprised to learn that the Distinguished Service Medal has already been struck with the minister's head on one side and the head of Seán na Sagart on the other.

'Catholic rights and Gaelic culture: for or against?'

To us a sacred trust is given. We are the connecting link between past generations of our great Catholic dead and the generations yet unborn. We are the spear-head of the far-flung empire of Erin's exiled sons and daughters. The honour, the great privilege, is ours and God helping us, we shall prove worthy of it. The issue is clearly knit – Catholic rights and Gaelic culture: for or against?'

Let there be no mealy mouthings about its sickening attributes in the twenty-six counties, where tolerance is synonymous with slavishness. North of the Boyne tolerance has a very different meaning. The minister thought he could insult the county with impunity, but we all stand honoured in that knowledge and we are ready to meet him and hand over the council to him, backed as he is by the powers of Freemasonry, which would not plead purely against the council. That council might soon be finished, but in relinquishing our positions we would tear Freemasonry from its roots, and how then would their little, prostituted government expect to survive? Personally I would welcome its political suicide as it dashed itself upon the rocks. [Loud applause]

Councillor Moclair opposed the selection of Miss Dunbar Harrison, describing the Local Appointments Commission procedure as flawed, like a game of 'Spoil Five'. The successful candidates who had Irish should have been chosen for service in Mayo. He claimed that Mayo had faced tyranny before and was now facing a tyranny of bureaucracy and despotism imposed on the County Council by the Minister for Local Government.

'The librarian,' Councillor Moclair said, 'may be designated the literary confessor of hundreds of young men and women who directly or indirectly must depend on her for guidance in reference to the type of books to be placed at their disposal. There may be some who may choose to lay down like beaten cowards and lick the hand that insults and rains blows on them. I refuse to be one of those and come what may I will fight against such tyranny to the bitter end.'

Councillor Peter Sweeney, a national-school teacher from Achill, did not agree with the library committee's stance with regard to Miss Dunbar Harrison's lack of Irish. He argued that if the passing of an examination in Irish was made an absolute qualification, very few appointments would be made in Mayo. Having said that, he was still going to oppose the employment of Miss Dunbar Harrison because the community needed to have confidence in their librarian.

'You have everyday dumped on our shores,' he said, 'shoals of communistic literature, sordid, vile literature.'[18]

The library committee would not be able to read everything so they would have to depend on the librarian and trust her decisions on what books she selected.

Councillor John McGeehin of Geesala said that had he not already made up his mind, the letter read by Councillor Bernard Joyce would have convinced him to oppose Miss Dunbar Harrison's appointment.

P.J. Ruttledge, a TD and vice-president of Fianna Fáil, 'tall, scholarly looking and unemotional',[19] declared that he and his colleague had been accused of intolerance by a certain paper.

'I am not here to parade toleration,' he said, 'but we do not stand for any religious bigotry.'[20] He opposed the methods of the Local Appointments Commission.

'A certain body of this council knows and I am very sorry the chairman has seen fit to stay away today, but there is a certain body of members here who knew a week ago that the [council] chairman [Michael Davis] was going to stay away. I am delighted Mr Chairman [Pat Higgins] that you have faced up to your responsibility but I always expected you would.'

The gallery cheered.

Thomas Campbell, Swinford, spoke initially in Irish, before switching to English. According to the *Roscommon Herald*, the solicitor 'addressed his remarks to the chairman as if he were endeavouring to bring a judge round to his view on a law point.'[21]

'When Miss Dunbar initially crosses the Shannon,' Mr Campbell said, 'as she probably will when we are wiped out as a council she will not shed the scales of Anglicisation. She has been nurtured in the school of anti-nationalism. She is admittedly ignorant of the national language, sent here by the minister that acted as chairman on the Gaeltacht Commission. So much for his consistency.'[22]

He then mentioned that a Swinford local, Bridge MacNulty, had applied for the position only to be told that 'she was not acceptable as she had no official experience of indexing and cataloguing in libraries, and all that sort of thing that could be learned by an office boy in two months.'

The gallery responded with jeers.

'This pretence that Miss Dunbar must make good when she comes down here, that she will reverse engines as it were, wipe out the past anti-nationalism and dedicate herself to the study of the Irish language, with great respect to Miss Dunbar, that cannot be more than a pretence. It would be absolutely impossible even with the best will in the world.'[23]

Seán Munnelly, Erris, 'one of the farmers' representatives, spoke briefly in pure Connaught Irish,'[24] opposing the acceptance of the recommendation of the Local Appointments Commission. Seán Ruane from Kiltimagh, yet another national-school teacher (he was also at the time president of the Connaught Council of the GAA), rose to his feet and explained that he had changed his position since the first meeting, as he had not known then that Irish was not a compulsory requirement for the job.

'It is not a religious issue,' he said. 'You have the opinions of certain distinguished ecclesiastics and I have my distinguished clergymen.'

'Name the clergymen,' countered Councillor Mullarkey.

'Name! Name!' came the chorus from the gallery.

'I will give them to you later.'

'Dean Conington of Swinford,' said Councillor Mellett.

'Yes, Dean Conington of Swinford, a man who had as distinguished a college course as any clergyman in Ireland.'

'And,' interjected Councillor Campbell, 'who received his national inspiration in a police barrack – in an RIC barrack.'

Cries of 'Oh' and much booing and howling issued from the gallery.

The chairman intervened. 'I don't think it is at all fair to this council to quote the private opinions of any individual.'

'We have been told that north of the Boyne is the place to look for bigotry. I am not one that condones the rampant bigotry there. It is wrong but we are not going to do the right thing by imitating it in the Free State. In the Free State the Catholic church is on a sound foundation and one more Protestant in Mayo is not going to upset the position and now as a result of this meeting the council will be dissolved. What great victory has been achieved?'

'That the people win,' replied Councillor Campbell.

'What great victory has been gained?' repeated Councillor Ruane. 'Quite a number of our boys from year to year have to go to England to work for Protestants. Some of our girls have to go to Scotland or America to work for Protestants and you are not making the position of these boys and girls any easier by taking the position several people have taken here today. By committing hari-kari we are putting the people of Mayo in a precarious position. I hold there is no religious principle involved.'

Dr Hardy, Fianna Fáil, Foxford, argued that no amount of excuses from the Cumann na nGaedheal councillors could explain away why they had changed their stance since the original meeting. 'The people of Mayo,' Dr Hardy said, 'when they have taken up a position, they stand by it honestly and honourably. Unfortunately, in the past certain people delivered bags of coal and flour to starving people to change their minds and make them do a thing which in their saner moments they would not do.'

'Your bludgeoning days'

Councillor Eamonn Moane, 'a farmers' representative, lean, wiry and athletic',[25] believed that the discussion had been unduly prolonged. He proceeded to criticise the statements of Councillor Ruane, who rose to respond.

'Sit down sir, I did not interrupt you. Sit down, sir! How dare you! Sit down!' shouted Councillor Moane.

'I will if I like,' replied the defiant Councillor Ruane.

'Sit down!'

'I will if the chairman orders me. Your bludgeoning days are over, Mr Moane.'[26]

'Bigger men than you have tried that, Mr Ruane.'

'I am only a small man.'

'This discussion has been carried on harmoniously up to this,' the chairman ruled. 'Let Mr Moane proceed.'

'In deference to your wish,' Councillor Ruane replied, 'I will sit down.'

'I apologise,' said Councillor Moane, 'to the chairman and the decent members of the council.'

'I spoke subject to correction,' insisted Councillor Ruane.

'I am correcting you now, sir!' said Councillor Moane.

'Do it respectfully!'

'I am correcting you now, and I defy contradiction from you.'

'Proceed, Mr Moane,' said the chairman.

'It might be as well if we reviewed the position,' said Councillor Moane. 'Unfortunately our people were stampeded a few years ago from the national position, otherwise the position we are in now would not have arisen. I say, and I do it without boasting, that I am one of those that have gone through a little at least and have done my part, and it has been successful if only for the issue that has at the present time, which affords the people an opportunity of striking at imperialism in this county a blow it never will recover from.'[27]

Councillor Moane sat down to applause from the gallery.

Councillor Mullarkey, Fianna Fáil, Ballindine, complained, 'If the chairman had taken my proposition to limit the speeches to three minutes, the meeting would be over long ago.'

'It was well worth our time hearing the speeches,' the chairman replied to widespread laughter.

'Shoddy English writers'

Councillor Mullarkey continued, 'The weakest argument I have heard is Mr Ruane's, that one more Protestant will not upset the position in Mayo. I am not opposed to the lady because she is a Protestant, but I feel she is not fit to take charge of the library in Gaeltacht Mayo. Would she prefer the works of Canon Sheehan and William O'Brien to shoddy English writers? I believe she would not. I agree with Thomas Davis in giving Protestants a chance. We gave Parnell a chance and were glad to give it. [Cheers]'[28]

There followed a procedural wrangle. Councillor Morahan announced that he had an addendum to move to Councillor O'Donnell's amendment. This proved to be a long and involved supplement. He asked Councillor O'Donnell did he agree to it and his response was that he did not understand it, which answer caused much laughter.[29]

'Are we to be kept here all day?' Councillor O'Hara complained.

'You cannot take an addendum to an amendment, it is out of order,' Councillor Walsh insisted.

'It is nearly time to end this controversy; I am nearly fainting with all the great speeching.'

'Manliness and manhood'

As the meeting neared its end, some laughter, much disorder and a degree of recrimination ensued.

'I say the clergymen who spoke already will be ashamed of the speeches that were made here today and of some of the men that made them,' Councillor O'Hara said. 'They would not go into a fifty-acre field with some of them.'[30]

The chairman intervened one last time, 'I am for over thirty years a member of public boards and I have never heard a finer display of eloquence, of patriotism, of manliness and manhood than I have heard here today [applause]. The discussion has been decorous and is fit to compare, in its ideas and ideals, with any other discussion carried out by any body within the four shores of Ireland.'

A division of the house was then taken. Councillor O'Hara's proposition that Miss Dunbar be appointed was put first.

For: J.P. O'Malley, J.T. Ruane, P. O'Hara, Giles Barrett, J.J. Duffy and J.A. Mellett (6).

Against: P.J. Ruttledge, T.S. Moclair, R. Walsh, P. Jordan, M.M. Nally, B. Joyce, T. Lavan, J.J. Mullarkey, P.S. Daly, J. Munnelly, J. Kilroy, J. McGeehin, Dr Hardy, T. Campbell, M. Kilroy, J.J. Honan, J.T. Morahan, E. Moane, M.H. O'Donnell, P. Sweeney, and the chairman, P. Higgins (21).

The amendment was then put as a resolution, with the same result. The announcement of the outcome was met by a great outburst of cheering and hand-clapping in the gallery. Shortly after the meeting first began the 'press representatives were passed a slip stating that twenty-one would vote against the appointment of the librarian and five for.'[31] The forecast was remarkably accurate, only one out, perhaps indicative of how opinions had hardened in Mayo in the previous weeks. Over the course of the three-hour debate eighteen of the attending councillors had spoken. There was little doubt that the result reflected public opinion in Mayo at the time. Recognising this, the Cumann na nGaedheal councillors who did not wish to oppose their own party took the diplomatic course and stayed away from the meeting. It was decided to telegraph the result to Richard Mulcahy and to the absent chairman of the council, Michael Davis. As the *Western People* put it, 'so ended the most momentous meeting of the Mayo County Council ever held.'[32]

The gallery was quickly evacuated. 'Sticking three hours of oratory was dry work and they all deserved a refresher.'[33] According to the *Roscommon Herald*'s correspondent, he was overwhelmed with invitations to join in the celebrations. 'Laughter and good cheer succeeded drama. Outside in the streets the Wren Boys cut curious capers and one of them played "Erin the Tear and the Smile in Thine Eyes". It was symbolical of the temperament of Mayo.'[34]

Chapter 7

'The recent unpleasantness'

Mayo County Council was abolished by ministerial order at the stroke of midnight on 31 December 1930. Mr P.J. Bartley took over as Commissioner in charge of County Mayo on 1 January 1931. An experienced local government official, he was well known in County Meath where he had had formerly been clerk of Oldcastle Union from 1908 to 1922. In 1922, after Independence, he was appointed inspector of registration at the Registrar-General. He left this position in 1931 to take up his new post in Mayo.

In 1904, according to the *Irish Independent*, P.J. Bartley had acted as honorary secretary of the 'first public open-air meeting held in Ireland at Finea to commemorate Myles the Slasher'. He was prominent in republican circles and was known to be a personal friend of Arthur Griffith. From 1901 to 1912 he was editor of a monthly magazine called *Sinn Féin*. It was rumoured that this was where the political party got the inspiration for its name: Sinn Féin – Ourselves Alone. What is undisputed is that he was a leading member of the new party. In 1905 he was elected as one of the five vice-presidents of Sinn Féin. Like many republicans he had been interred in Ballykinlar Camp from 1920 to 1921. The *Irish Independent* reported that he was proud of his time spent as clerk of Oldcastle Union. 'During his period of office he had the satisfaction of never having had a single surcharge against the guardians.'[1]

The *Cork Examiner* headlined their report, 'Minister Defied – Mayo Will Not Have Librarian – Council's Decision Not to be Browbeaten by Threats.'[2] The *Western People* informed its readership that the commissioner had taken up residence in McEllin's Hotel, Balla, perhaps implying that P.J. Bartley did not expect it to be a long-term engagement in Mayo. Dissolution of councils was neither unusual nor unprecedented at the time. In the 1920s it had been a commonly used tool of central government. The Civil War had in some areas led to widespread administrative disorder in the local authorities. Some 'local bodies had ceased to hold meetings and rate collection lapsed.'[3] Both Kerry and Leitrim County Councils had been dissolved in 1923. Dublin and Cork corporations followed in 1924. 'A total of twenty bodies were replaced by commissioners in the first three years of the new state.'[4]

P.J. Bartley was all business at the commissioner's first meeting. The proceedings lasted all of twenty-five minutes. Only the clerical and survey staff of the council attended, together with four members of the general public and one former councillor. Commissioner Bartley administered £75,000 worth of public works, which one local newspaper accurately calculated to be a spending rate of £3,000 a minute. He heard a deputation from Lahardan in regard to a road and he appointed a caretaker for Hollymount courthouse. He then formally appointed Miss Dunbar Harrison as Mayo county librarian.

The *Leitrim Observer* seemed impressed by this speedy work. 'The roads meeting last year,' it wrote, 'lasted from 10 a.m. to 7 p.m. and the matter was further discussed at three subsequent meetings.'[5] *The Connaught Telegraph* was equally taken with him. According to its reporter, 'Even the very air of the chamber was inspired with a commissioner-like spirit of business.' The meeting began at 11 a.m. and was over before 11.30 a.m.

'That completes the business,' Mr M.J. Egan remarked.

'It will be a half-holiday for the press today,' Bartley jokingly announced as he was leaving the council chamber. Perhaps it was this that impressed them.[6]

'The nabobs at Dublin'

Not all the local papers were as welcoming towards Commissioner

Bartley. The *Mayo News* argued 'better this open and unabashed tyranny – taxation without representation – than the so-called local government which, hamstrung and powerless, has been in existence since the nabobs at Dublin robbed local representatives of all power to manage local affairs.'[7] A week later the *Mayo News* was no more reconciled to the newly installed librarian. 'Who can stop Mr Mulcahy from appointing the Trinity College shoneen?'[8] It was this level of hostility that Miss Dunbar Harrison was about to confront.

Resentment of Trinity College was widespread and blatant within nationalist and republican circles in the Free State. Trinity served as a handy shorthand for the West-British, loyalist, unionist, royalist and Freemason ascendancy; it was a remnant of the recently defeated enemy that remained a potent bogeyman to be evoked as required. There was also an element of class envy in the enmity displayed. For some, the equation of Catholicism with Irishness was so obvious it hardly needed stating. The two were virtually interchangeable. As was Protestantism with Englishness, and Trinity was a badge of Protestantism.

The hostility to Trinity and all it represented was a feature of 'respectable' Catholic opinion in the 1920s and 1930s. As one historian put it: 'In 1927 the Catholic hierarchy reaffirmed its opposition to Catholics attending Trinity College, Dublin. Interestingly, there was no such antipathy towards Catholics attending Queen's University Belfast.'[9] Some Catholic priests did speak out against attendance at Queen's, but the hostility shown towards this university was much less than that aimed at Trinity. Perhaps the Catholic clergy were showing their pragmatic side, realising that Queen's was the only real third-level outlet for Catholics in the North and that any ban they put on it would be largely ignored.

As ever the *Catholic Bulletin* could be relied upon to take an extreme view. It questioned whether a Catholic graduate of Trinity could be trusted. 'Is not the title of Catholic, assumed and used by a Catholic medical graduate of Trinity College, Dublin, simply an added danger for our Catholic population, rich and poor?'[10]

The new county librarian was quoted in the *Irish Independent* on 5 January 1931, as intending to travel to Mayo at the earliest opportunity. She hoped that the recent unpleasantness would be forgotten. 'I shall do my utmost,' she remarked, 'to make a success of my job, and I hope I shall have the good will and co-operation of everybody interested in the library scheme. I shall always have the best interests of Mayo at heart, and its people I will endeavour to serve faithfully and well.'[11]

Letitia Dunbar was born in Dundrum, Dublin, on 4 February 1906. Her parents emigrated to the United States with the rest of her immediate family but she remained in Ireland.[12] As was not that unusual at the time, she was given into the care of her mother's sister, Edith Elizabeth Harrison, and Edith's husband, John Walter Harrison of 72 Palmerston Road, Dublin. In later life she took their name.

The 1911 census lists the Harrison family address as 60 Clondalkin. John Harrison's occupation was recorded as warehouseman. The family was prosperous enough to have a live-in cook/domestic servant. Their religion was Church of Ireland. The then five-year-old Aileen Letitia was recorded on the form as the niece of Edith and John Harrison and given their surname. She was educated at Alexandra School in Dublin from 1918 to 1922, where she received honours in the Junior Grade, Intermediate, and won the Jeannie Turpin Essay Prize and the Helen Prenter Prize in English Literature. In 1922 she attended Alexandra College where she secured the Lady Ardilaun Entrance Scholarship in French. Having passed the Middle and Senior Grade Intermediate in 1924 she was one of only a few women at the time to enter Trinity College. In 1928 she graduated with honours in modern languages (French and Spanish). After graduation she took a course in library training in the Dublin County Library Headquarters at

Kilmainham. She spent six months in the library headquarters before continuing on to Rathmines Public Library where she took charge of the children's library and gave lectures to the children for a period of nine months. She also attended a library-training summer course at University College Dublin.

Miss Dunbar Harrison took the name of her uncle's family and was variously known as Letitia Dunbar, Letitia Harrison or Letitia Dunbar Harrison. She formally changed her surname to Harrison by deed poll at the time that the Mayo librarian controversy blew up.

In an interview in the *Western People*, one of Miss Dunbar Harrison's main opponents, Dean D'Alton, stated that 'the government have fallen into a pit of their own making, and are finding themselves in an awkward as well as an unpopular position, which will probably lead to their undoing.' Asked by the reporter if the library committee would continue to act after the advent of the commissioner, Dean D'Alton said he believed they would not. It was his expectation too, that voluntary helpers in the local library centres would also decline to continue their work and would send back the books they had in stock.

'The whole affair is regrettable,' the Dean concluded.[13]

Chapter 8

'Low fellowship and bad habits'

In the early years of the Free State the development of county-wide library services was still in its infancy. In the previous decades Andrew Carnegie, as a personal gift, contributed financial support to the establishment of libraries in Ireland. He offered grants to fund the library buildings and once the money had been paid over he ceased to have any connection with the library authority.[1] Library growth in Ireland was a haphazard area, very much dependent on organisations or individuals with the knowledge and initiative to apply to Carnegie for funding.

Andrew Carnegie had made vast sums of money in America as a steel manufacturer. In later years he became involved in charitable works, principally in giving financial support to the building of libraries. According to Mr Carnegie himself, he had spent a great deal of time in a library during his youth and it had both instilled in him a love of literature and 'steered him clear of low fellowship and bad habits.' Not only that, it had also revealed to him 'the precious treasures of knowledge and imagination through which youth can ascend.'[2]

After the Carnegie Trust was set up in 1913, an Irish committee was established and the writer Lennox Robinson was appointed organiser. As Lennox Robinson himself confessed, 'When I was appointed manager and producer at the Abbey Theatre I knew nothing of stage work; in this case I knew nothing of library work. But the appointment was not quite insane, not as insane as the Abbey one.'[3] Robinson was of the opinion that much of Andrew Carnegie's original financial support of libraries had been in vain. 'His benefactions were generous and well-meaning but often ill-judged ... I believe Mr Jack Yeats once painted a picture of an Irish village hiding behind a hill to try to escape a library.'[4] The Trust decided to change its policy. Previously it had concentrated on a library-building programme. It was decided to spend less on buildings and more on administration and also to 'keep a certain amount of friendly control and supervision over library schemes for some years.'[5] It was felt they could get better value for their money by supplying books, equipment and administration rather than just buildings. The result was the rural library movement. The aim became 'books and buildings, books for the villages and townlands, for the schools, village clubs, the family and the individual student.'[6]

Numerous small communities managed 'to secure a small building which they boldly named a library but the "librarian" was only a badly paid caretaker and there were few or no books.' Many of the original Carnegie libraries fell into disrepair due to a lack of funding for their maintenance and upkeep. The Trust recognised that there was a particular problem when it came to rural counties. The secretary of the United Kingdom Carnegie Trust highlighted the challenge facing large remote areas. 'In the county,' he said, 'the essential fact is that no matter how much you might like to have a big central library, you can never place it near enough to all the people to make it genuinely accessible.'[7] It was this problem that led to a change of emphasis in the Trust's grants from fixed buildings, which by their nature tended to be located in urban areas, to book stock that could be moved around from library to library and region to region.

According to a 1929 report by the Library Association of Ireland, there was still great room for improvement. 'The shortcomings of libraries in Ireland was due to one main cause – poverty.'[8] One of the problems was that 'it was clear that in the majority of cases Mr Carnegie's grants had been given without very complete knowledge of local conditions ...' and many of the original library buildings had fallen into disuse.

The Local Government Act of 1925 made county councils the new unit of rural library administration. They were given the power to levy a library rate thus permitting them to become statutory library authorities. Within the next decade 'county followed county in rapid succession' in setting up a library scheme, and by 1935 only Longford and Westmeath were without a service.[9] The Carnegie trustees continually reminded the local authorities of 'the necessity of appointing only professionally skilled librarians and of paying salaries commensurate with the position.'[10] The Trust made it a condition attached to their grants that the librarian should be paid not less than £250 a year.

The library service that Miss Dunbar Harrison was set to inherit had only a short existence. Like most county libraries it was a recent innovation and had only been set up in 1926 by Miss Dunbar Harrison's immediate predecessor and Mayo's first county librarian, Miss Brigid Redmond. Mayo County Council had hesitated for eighteen months before finally deciding to accept a grant from the Carnegie Trust to establish a county-circulating library. The councillors were divided, with 'one section eager to welcome the gift of free books for the people, another fearful lest the promised gift should mask a dangerous weapon of imperialistic propaganda.'[11]

In its early formative years the Irish Free State tended to look inwards, with a pronounced protectionist attitude, especially with regard to social and moral matters. Censorship was one by-product of this desire to shelter the citizens of the new state from the baleful influence of the outside world. The Catholic church in Ireland was especially wary of external influences. Libraries could be dangerous places, and librarians could be the means by which innocent people might become infected by dangerous and subversive ideas such as Communism. The following 1931 Lenten pastoral of Rev. Dr Finnegan is a typical example of this attitude:

It is said that thirty tons of literature, consisting principally of the scandals of the world, reach this country every week. If this literature be read in such quantities it will very soon undermine both the morals and the faith of the people. It is also stated that there are circulating, weekly, in Ireland, twenty papers of this dangerous description.

Since my last Lenten letter, steps have been taken to establish a public library in the counties of Cavan and Leitrim. If carefully and cautiously managed, these may become a means of instruction, enlightenment and even of edification. They do require cautious management. The greater number of the books must necessarily come from publishers outside Ireland. It is a well-known fact that literature subversive of faith and morals issues in great quantities from the English press. Should such literature to any extent get into them, the public libraries, instead of a blessing, would become a curse.[12]

'Dismissed I was'

It was unfortunate that during this period of expansion, Lennox Robinson, who was the Trust's organiser in Ireland, fell foul of the country's moral guardians. One of his literary endeavours stirred up a controversy in 1924. Robinson contributed a short story on a religious theme, written many years previously, to a literary paper edited by Francis Stuart. 'The Madonna of Slieve Dun' was a mild enough tale, a slice of rural miserabilism about a young, naïve and religious country girl, Mary Creedon, who imagines herself to be another Blessed Virgin come to save the town of Liscree from the wickedness of drinking, gambling and horse-racing, but on publication it caused outrage. 'A first-rate row blew up' when W.B. Yeats got involved.[13] As Mr Robinson himself put it, 'On account of my story a Catholic cleric resigned from the Carnegie advisory committee. He was important and strongly backed by the provost … my resignation was demanded. I refused it. I preferred to be dismissed and after a lot of haggling and trying to save everyone's face, dismissed I was. The whole thing was inexpressively painful to me. It alienated many of my Catholic friends and with some the breach will never be healed.'[14]

To suspicious minds this incident raised yet another question mark over the motives of the Carnegie Trust; its organiser in Ireland was seen as a purveyor of blasphemous yarns. Despite these vicissitudes, the Trust continued its work in Ireland throughout the 1920s, concentrating mainly on the previously neglected country areas. Its scheme for rural library services treated a county as one unit with centralised control and a circulating book system. This type of plan had proved quite successful in England and was now being tried out in many Irish counties. As the county librarian for Dublin described it, 'The chief characteristic of these county library schemes is a central distributing depot, from which books are sent out to small centres in schools and village halls or small town libraries and changed every three months.'[15] Operating through these modest centres a negligible outlay of funding could provide a basic library service over a large area.

The choice of location for these distribution centres was crucial. Dermot Foley's experiences in Clare could be regarded as typical. 'A school, especially if it stood near a church,' he said, 'was the only choice in rural parts, and a corner shop or post office was the best bet in villages. A few towns had a club hall, but the trouble there was that every conceivable group used it, from tin-whistle bands to snooker players to card schools, so chicken-wired frames to protect the books at all times, except for an hour or two in the week set aside for the library, had to be made.'[16] Some counties came up with more innovative solutions. At least one library centre was based in a pub; it was run by a Mr T. Moran in Drumshambo.[17] This type of haphazard organisation, which was almost entirely dependent on voluntary help, worked surprisingly well. Roísín Walsh, Dublin county librarian, expressed the doubts she initially felt. 'You cannot believe,' she said, 'that books passing through the hands of untrained workers in small centres to rural readers in remote corners of the county will ever find their way back to the haven of headquarters again. Strange to say, your fears are quite unfounded, for the books come back, up to time, and certainly looking no worse than if they had been circulating for the same period in a highly respectable suburb.'[18]

In July 1925 the Carnegie Trust wrote to all the county councils who had not set up a library service, intimating that their offer of grants would be withdrawn in December 1930, after which date no further grants would be available.[19] Essentially the Trust was setting a deadline for these tardy councils to avail of their funding. There was, however, a certain residual distrust of the motives of a foreign body funding services in Ireland, despite the Trust's apparently philanthropic roots. During the often acrimonious debates in Leitrim, Councillor Pat Kilkenny asserted that he was against the adoption of the Public Libraries Act in his county as 'old Carnegie was an Englishman and he made all his money in America on the sweat of the workers.'[20] Carnegie, of course, was of Scottish descent but suspicion of his motives remained a political fact in much of rural, conservative Ireland.

Councillor Kilkenny from Aughavas had strong views on libraries. He was of the view that 'books were alright in their own way but it would be better to give the starving people of the countryside bags of flour than start lumping volumes on them.'[21] Many local councillors were hostile to libraries simply because in the long run they would have to pay for them. They believed there were more needy projects deserving of their scarce funding. The Clare experience was not untypical. Dermot Foley was told by one politician of the agricultural persuasion, ''Tisn't a book a man should have in his hands, Mister Librarian, but a pair of horses. Three years I'm looking for a grant to build a shed for the cattle. I was to find that the Clare County Council could breed more non-sequiturs in one season than a dog has fleas.'[22] Some councillors were also sceptical of who would use the service. 'It is all very well to be talking about literature,' Councillor James Creamer of Ballinamore asserted, 'but if those who advocate it had to go into a gripe or a ditch to earn a living it would be a different matter. Shopkeepers who have an easy way of making money, and others who are gorged with big salaries, may be in favour of it, but I say it is an outrage and intolerable on the ratepayers to bring it forward now.' Councillor Michael McGrath from Carrick-on-Shannon was equally unconvinced with regard to the literary interests of his county people. 'I think all who are conversant with this subject,' he said, 'know that the library will serve about two dozen people in County Leitrim.'[23]

'Westwards to Mayo'

Brigid Redmond was appointed the first county librarian of Mayo in 1926. The library scheme was to be under probation for a period of two years, financed by the Carnegie Trust. If at the end of that period, the scheme was found to be successful, it would be adopted by the County Council, and a rate would be struck for the permanent maintenance of the library service. Essentially, Brigid Redmond was a pioneer setting out into uncharted territory, and that certainly seems to be how she felt. As she herself described it, 'One grim November day I left the cheery homelights of Dublin behind and went westwards to Mayo.'[24]

Her first task was to secure premises for the new library service. Two towns had contended for the honour of housing the headquarters – Claremorris and Ballinrobe. Miss Redmond inspected the Claremorris building first. It was situated about a mile outside of the town, 'in the middle of a windy desolate plain … the disused workhouse and fever hospital. Here the council had indicated certain rooms which might be used for the purpose of a library. As I looked round the dank walls and through the bleak deserted passages, I fancied that I could hear the sad plaints of the Famine victims in the weird moaning of the wind sweeping down the chimneys and out through the creaking, barred windows. "Ye'd have no neighbours here but the rats, Miss," remarked the caretaker. I agreed and fled precipitately to Ballinrobe.'[25]

Miss Redmond found Ballinrobe much more congenial, though again the site on offer was somewhat unsuitable. 'Here the kindly hospitality and warm welcome of Monsignor D'Alton almost inclined me to pitch my tent in the available rooms at the workhouse.'[26] This seems to have been a common theme for these rural library services, the offering of big, old, buildings in some state of disrepair. In Laois, as the new librarian told it, 'The council placed some rooms in the old gaol at our disposal – rooms at the time but slightly removed from the amenities offered to those about to die or be transported under the laws of "the good old days".'[27]

Brigid Redmond decided to reject Ballinrobe as the site for the library. The town suffered from its position at the southern extremity of the county, close to the border with Galway, which Miss Redmond said made it 'unsuitable for the operation of a scheme which involved the service of the whole county. Yet, I could not help regretting my departure from the dear little town by the Robe with its pleasant shady walks and its beautiful church with the procession of Irish saints shining in a glory of rich, flaming colours from the grey walls.'[28] Instead it was decided to request that the County Council provide accommodation for the county book repository in Castlebar courthouse. Two rooms were found there and given up to the library committee, which was 'presided over by the Most Rev. Dr Naughton, Bishop of Killala, and it included some of the highest ecclesiastics and leading men of the county.'[29]

The early months saw Miss Redmond busy preparing the first few thousand books chosen for inclusion from lists which she had submitted to the book-selection committee, together with additional lists forwarded by people anxious to take charge of local branches. Dean D'Alton and Canon Hegarty were among those who served on the book-selection committee, which comprised thirty-eight members. The Local Government Act of 1925 allowed county councils to delegate virtually all of their responsibilities regarding the library service to a library committee. The two significant exceptions – powers that could not be delegated and had to be retained by the full council – were the levying of the library rate and the borrowing of money. By and large the politicians regarded library provision as a specialist service so they were only too happy to divest themselves of the responsibility and leave the day-to-day running of the scheme to a librarian, while a library committee supervised the overall running of the service.[30] In general, the duties of a county library committee could be boiled down to a couple of phrases, 'The librarian advises; the committee decides. The committee sets the course; the librarian steers it.'[31]

'Crazy ... unaisy ... lazy'

The relationship between the chairman of the committee and the county librarian could be crucial. 'On his [the chairman's] tact, imperturbability, and good judgement depend the good relations which should exist between librarian and committee.' As one veteran library committee member put it, not entirely seriously one presumes, the function of the chairman involved 'checking the crazy ones, soothing the unaisy ones and keeping the lazy ones from falling asleep.'[32]

Of the initial book stock selected in Mayo, Miss Redmond commented, 'Most of the books were of national interest: Irish history, biography, economics, stories of Irish life and books in the Irish language.' Miss Redmond relied heavily on the clergy to publicise the new service. '[They] spoke to the people on Sundays about the scheme,' she said, 'and arranged meetings after mass, at which committees were organised for the establishment of local libraries.'

Ballina was one of the first branches to open. 'Twice a week the library was open to the people – on market days and Sundays, when it was served by voluntary library helpers.'[33] Unpaid helpers were vital to the long-term survival of these tiny libraries. As Dermot Foley in Clare explained, 'The worst problem was finding a voluntary librarian. I learned to be slow accepting policemen's wives, who, though always reliable, were regarded as strangers to the parish and likely to carry significant pieces of information into the barracks.'[34] He went on to reveal that on one occasion he had hoped to make a certain postman a helper until the gentleman concerned told him that he had a prejudice against any book that began with the personal pronoun, 'I'. Such were the cares and woes of a county librarian in rural Ireland.

The Swinford library committee was so anxious to secure a branch that when a new courthouse was being built in the town they took care to have the architect include a 'special room for library purposes ... At Killala, the parish priest took a kindly, practical interest in the welfare of the library ... providing the equipment free of cost.'[35] Miss McMahon, a Dublin lady living in Keel, Achill, 'in the midst of all her work, found time to interest herself in the library and introduced branches into five districts of Achill.' In Kiltimagh, 'the Sisters of St Louis undertook the charge of the branch, for the people of the town.' An energetic teacher established a library branch in Tourmakeady and 'formed a students' reading circle for the study of Irish literature.' While in Foxford, 'the nun in charge was delighted to add the collection of new books from the library to her store.'[36]

Even the most remote of districts could avail of the service. Killeadan had a small library established as did Ballintubber. In one wild district Miss Redmond recounted, 'a tall gaunt Scotsman kept a shop beside a cross-roads, and had charge of a collection of books.' Miss Redmond went as far as to set up a scheme for the inhabitants of Clare Island. 'At all events,' she said, 'they were delighted to get the library books for which they sent over a boat every six months.'[37] In Castlebar, the local library committee established their town library in the Pioneer Hall. They also applied for 'a special collection of non-fiction books for the use of the Men's Club.'[38]

Once the service was launched, 'every district in the county clamoured for books. Collections of Irish ballads, speeches, folklore, sets of plays, some in Irish, some in English, books on cattle diseases, poultry-keeping and agriculture, books of a religious nature all proved popular. There was an ever-increasing demand for books with an Irish-Ireland outlook, books dealing with national history, biography, economics.'[39] The library stock was advertised through articles in the local papers, by circulating lists of books held on different subjects and also 'by book exhibits held at the local feiseanna.' Miss Redmond described how 'the library became an enquiry bureau as well as a book repository. People came here with all sorts of queries ranging from the best method of treating swine fever or the warble fly pest, to queries on trade-marks, land acts, egg-testers, and dry fly fishing.'[40]

'The counter attractions of Gaelic football and step dancing'

In Laois the library service had 'a stall at the Upper Ossory Agricultural Show ... and a display of Irish texts at the Feis Mhór held under the auspices of the Gaelic League. The latter was not very successful as the counter attractions of Gaelic football and step dancing, not to mention coconut shies and "Find the Lady", overshadowed the literary claims ...'[41]

Miss Redmond's library committee 'included thirty-eight members, from all parts of the county.' She claimed it was 'thoroughly representative, and took a lively interest in the library.'[42] While it may have been thoroughly representative, it was also undoubtedly true that members of the Catholic clergy were the dominant force.

As was patently obvious, Letitia Dunbar Harrison was in a much more difficult position as county librarian than Brigid Redmond had been. Given all that had taken place prior to her arrival, she would have great difficulty building up a relationship with the members of the old library committee in County Mayo. Her only option was to reconstitute a different working group. However, this was problematic since there was talk that the Catholic clergy who had acted on the previous committee would refuse to serve under the new regime. Not only that, it was also rumoured that they were urging other local notables not to co-operate with the new regime. The spectre of a clerically organised boycott of Mayo's library service had been raised.

Brigid Redmond's time in Mayo was relatively short. She resigned as county librarian in February 1930, reportedly as a result of a clash of personalities with the Mayo county secretary, M.J. Egan. The County Council had received a letter from a civil servant in the Department of Local Government complaining about her lack of efficiency. This mysterious letter was later rescinded on the grounds that the individual concerned (the scribe of said letter) did not have the authority to send it.

Rural library services were almost entirely dependent on the voluntary, unpaid helpers who ran the library centres. As a 1935 report put it, 'In counties of scattered population it is reasonable to expect the number of small centres to be relatively greater than in counties where there are a number of populous areas.' Country-wide, in the Free State, roughly 2,350 library centres were being run by the local authorities. They were located mainly in schools and parish halls. Of these, 2,282 were run by unpaid workers and over 100 were situated in Mayo. The vast majority were very small, had an average of little more than one hundred books in stock at any one time and opened for a very limited number of hours.[43]

'Expediency, efficiency and economy'

The rapidly expanding library service was still at an early stage of development. As Christina Keogh put it, 'No other branch of the public service has received more external financial assistance or a lesser measure of internal financial support ... The soul of the scheme was expediency, efficiency and economy; unfortunately, too keen a pursuance of economy has rather impeded the acquisition of the other two qualities.'[44]

Brigid Redmond continued her career as county librarian in Wicklow. On her departure from Mayo, the County Council assigned a Mr Hamrock as a temporary replacement. The library committee promptly resigned, claiming they had not been consulted in the appointment. Clearly there was much unrest in the Mayo library service, even before the announcement of Miss Dunbar Harrison's success.

Miss Dunbar Harrison arrived in Castlebar during the second week in January. As the *Mayo News* reported, 'On Wednesday morning Miss Dunbar took up duty. She showed a definite desire in her capacity to act as librarian without any patronage from any section of the community. The feeling in the town is decidedly friendly towards her, and those strongest in opposition to the appointment make it clear that as far as she is concerned personally, she has their good wishes.'[45]

Despite Miss Redmond's troubles in Mayo, she had succeeded in setting up a sturdy and extensive library service in the county. By the time of Miss Dunbar Harrison's appointment there were over one hundred active library centres in operation. Many had been launched and were still being maintained with the support of the local Catholic clergy. Without their continued co-operation, could these libraries survive?

Chapter 9

'Unwept, unhonoured and unsung'

If the government hoped that the dissolution of the council and the appointment of Miss Dunbar Harrison by Commissioner Bartley would bring an end to the political controversy, they were proved mistaken. In the immediate aftermath of the special meeting of the council, the government felt it necessary to rebut the claims of a letter written by an unidentified unsuccessful candidate. Councillor Bernard Joyce had dramatically read this letter aloud at the meeting. Accounts of its contents were widely publicised in national and regional newspapers. In order to protect the good name of the Local Appointments Commission, the accusations in the letter needed to be tackled directly.

In a further development, the anonymous letter writer gave permission for her name and address to be published. She was revealed to be Miss Ellen Burke, with an address at Bank House, Longford. Her epistle, the exact text of which Councillor Joyce had written into the minutes of the meeting of Mayo County Council, was printed in its entirety in most of the national dailies and the regional weekly newspapers, together with an explanatory covering letter from Dean D'Alton. The covering letter read as follows:

Sir,

The letter read at the Mayo Council meeting, on Saturday, had been handed by me to our local county councillor, Mr Joyce, and it was read without giving the writer's name and address. Since then I have got full authority to publish both the name and address of the writer, and I will ask you to publish the letter in full in the interests of fair play and in justice to a young lady who has been wronged.

I make no comment, except to point out that this young lady, Miss Burke, when the appointment as librarian was made, had already reached the required age, had the diploma in library training, and had plenty of Irish even for a Gaeltacht county. Not one of these qualifications was possessed by her successful opponent, Miss Dunbar.

E. A. D'Alton,
Parish Priest, LL. D., Dean of Tuam,
St Mary's, Ballinrobe

Ellen Burke's letter read as follows.

Dear Canon D'Alton,

I have just received a letter from Fr Brown, SJ, instructing me to write to you with reference to Mayo library. I was called before the Appointments Commission when they selected librarians for the last group of libraries, including Mayo, and, much to the surprise of my professors, was passed over.

I received a good secondary education in St Louis Convent, Balla, Loreto Convent, Killarney, and Dominican College, Eccles St, Dublin. I passed Junior and Middle Grade Intermediate and Matriculation (N.U.I.) I am a Bachelor of Commerce and have the Higher Diploma in Education and the Diploma in Library Training of the National University of Ireland. I passed an oral and written examination in Irish for my B. Comm. Degree, and have had the advantage of spending my holidays in the Kerry Gaeltacht for the past five years.

I did a considerable amount of practical work in University College Library in preparation for the Library Diploma, as I gave whole-time attention to library training all through the year. I did practical library work in the Catholic Central Library from the beginning of February until the end of June last. I attended daily at Kilmainham Library under the supervision of Miss R. [Roísín] Walsh, county librarian.

When I had completed one week's practical work in Kilmainham I was called before the Appointments Commission, but I told the examiners I intended continuing my work in Kilmainham for two months, and I did so. I was twenty-five years of age last April, and so had reached the required age. I am also a Catholic.

Ellen Burke,
Bank House, Longford, 22 December 1930[1]

Fr Stephen Brown, who Miss Burke mentioned as her mentor, was the librarian of the Catholic Central Library where Miss Burke had worked for roughly five months. He was also an active member of the Library Association of Ireland. Dean D'Alton speaking to the *Western People* said that it was surprising, in view of all her attainments, that Miss Burke had not been selected for the position. Moreover, she was a Catholic and Mayo was a predominantly Catholic county.[2]

Up to this time, the internal actions of the Local Appointments Commission and its interview boards had been treated as confidential. They had at all times acted independently of the government. It is a sign of the pressure that he was under that President Cosgrave, acting on the advice of the attorney general, formally asked the LAC for a response to the Ellen Burke letter. It was felt that the government had no option but to reply. To not have done so and to let such a devastating accusation go unanswered would have been politically disastrous. Considering the time of year, the Local Appointments Commissioners responded with some alacrity, and by 5 January 1931 the office of the president had received a written report from the Commission which formally rebutted each of the points in Miss Ellen Burke's letter.

1) The statements in the letter of the candidate as to her education, training and experience were correct.

2) All those statements with regard to her education, training and experience were all before the selection board when they interviewed her.

3) The selection board was aware of all the circumstances of Miss Burke's career, as set out in her letter.

4) The Local Appointments Commissioners, after considering the report of the board of selection, which did not place Miss Burke on the list of qualified candidates, were satisfied that the interview board had taken fully into account all the facts and circumstances above referred to as to Miss Burke's career and qualifications and had exercised all due care in assessing her merits and those of the other candidates.

5) If anything to suggest the need for doing so had presented itself, the board would have been invited to review their assessment.

6) As regards knowledge of Irish, Miss Burke had not reached the standard.

> 7) As in the case of other applicants, the commissioners were not aware of, or concerned with the religion of Miss Burke.[3]

One can only imagine the grim satisfaction, or at the very least immense relief, of the cabinet. Ellen Burke had, despite her declarations to the contrary, failed the Irish test as well as the interview proper. If this was the sole basis for the opposition to Miss Letitia Dunbar Harrison, it was on feeble grounds. Miss Burke had shown astonishing naïvety. To put it at its mildest, she had been badly advised. By going public, she had allowed herself to be used as a pawn in a political game. The government could not be seen to back away from such a public challenge to their integrity. To add emphasis and with a certain harsh inevitability, it was later revealed that Ellen Burke had previously gone before another selection board for a county librarian post with a different set of interviewers. She had also been unsuccessful on that occasion. The government felt its hand had been strengthened. They could now put up a more robust defence of the Local Appointments Commission than had seemed possible a few days earlier. They were in a position to cut the ground from under Ellen Burke and those who were backing her.

In the formal and semi-formal meetings with various members of the Catholic hierarchy in the following weeks and months, the contents of the report of the Local Appointments Commissioners were made available to them. These so-called confidential government papers were widely if informally disseminated. The campaign in favour of Miss Burke was quietly dropped. This did not, of course, mean that the argument for the acceptance of Miss Dunbar Harrison had been made. The debate in the letters pages of the newspapers showed no sign of abating. Unlike current practice, it was not uncommon for letters to be published under a pseudonym if the writer so wished. It was, perhaps, easier to support minority opinions if one did not have to sign a name to the letter. In one particular letter a 'Clareman' declared, 'It is with great pleasure that Irish Catholics in England will read of the government's action in resisting local bigotry in Mayo and insisting on the appointment of the elected candidate, although a Protestant ... If the forces of reaction in Mayo succeed in their effort to flout the law of the Free State, it looks as if Ireland is not yet fit for self-government.'[4]

The Labour Party's weekly magazine, *The Watchword*, was broadly supportive. 'From beginning to end,' it wrote, 'the affair of the Mayo librarianship reflects little credit on the majority of the Mayo County Council. At the sworn inquiry conducted by the Local Government Department before Christmas the council officially put forward the case that its objection to the appointment of Miss Dunbar was based on the ground that she had not a sufficiently good knowledge of Irish. But the lay and clerical leaders of the campaign against the appointment have been guilty of no such hypocrisy. They have maintained openly and frankly all along that their chief objection is against Miss Dunbar's religion.'[5] *The Watchword* declared its regret that the council had to be dissolved, 'In future some provision other than the appointment of a commissioner should be made for cases such as these. The affair will not end even with the ratification of Miss Dunbar's appointment. The campaign which has been waging for the last month will not cease ... We anticipate that steps will be taken to make the librarian's position a very heavy burden indeed.'[6]

The political combat continued into the New Year. In early January 1931 the Fianna Fáil newspaper *The Nation* carried the headline 'Mayo Council To Go'. It wrote, 'The story will go around the world that to secure the appointment of a Protestant to a public post the Free State government has to suppress the principal elected local assembly.'[7] The paper seemed to be blaming Cumann na nGaedheal for damaging the Free State's reputation abroad. Indeed the controversy did cause ripples abroad though mainly among Irish exiles.

'Inverted Ku Klux Klanism'

Daniel Maloney, with an address at 362 St Mark's Place, Staten Island, New York, wrote to the *Western People*.

As an Irishman interested in the good name of Ireland and her repute, not merely for unconditional tolerance in matters concerning the expression of opinion, but for courtesy and good will, I was inexpressibly shocked to read of a candidate for the post of librarianship being discriminated against because of her religion and university. This action is nothing short of inverted Ku Klux Klanism and no civilised community would for a moment tolerate a library committee capable of this perversion of their office.

If your great county man, Michael Davitt, were now living he would stigmatise this petty bigotry as a blow at Irish culture, Irish democracy, Irish nationality and Irish unity. In our twentieth century such news travels fast and injures the name of Mayo throughout the civilised world.

Burning issues press for solution in our day and public bodies who waste public time not only by failing to meet these issues, but by maliciously dragging in ridiculous theological prejudices into matters of education and justice, are unworthy representatives of Mayo.[8]

In fact Mayo man Michael Davitt had held strong views on libraries. In his book *Leaves from a Prison Diary*, written while serving his sentence in Dartmoor for treason felony, he wrote, 'In my opinion, no more efficacious reforming medium ... could be employed for the reclamation of all that is reclaimable in criminal lives than a judiciously stocked prison library ... Half a prison library might be stocked with biographies of self-made and remarkable men, the struggles and achievements of whose lives would constitute the best class of reading that could be offered to those who, above everything else, stand in need of instruction by example.' Michael Davitt deplored the religious prejudice shown in much of the stock of English prison libraries. 'It is a pity,' he wrote, 'that sectarianism is so often displayed in their pages that the Catholic chaplains of convict prisons interdict their delivery to Catholic prisoners.'[9]

As the letter writer from New York put it, one can only imagine Michael Davitt's reaction to the sectarianism shown in his native county. As for Fianna Fáil, its leader Eamon de Valera gave his views on 6 January at a public meeting in Irishtown, County Mayo, close to the birthplace of Michael Davitt. Replying to a questioner from among a crowd of nearly two thousand people, who asked him to describe his attitude to what had happened, Mr de Valera said that although he had not intended to speak on it he was prepared to state his opinion. Fianna Fáil had opposed the Local Appointments Commission from the outset, believing that 'centralisation of power in Dublin was a mistake, as the same intelligence could be found in county councils.'[10] Centralisation was not only unnecessary but it was also inadvisable because the people of Dublin had enough work of their own to do and he thought they should let others shoulder their share of the work and responsibility. He went on to state that, although he had not been aware of it at the time, he heartily approved of Fianna Fáil's opposition on the County Council to Miss Dunbar Harrison's appointment, on the basis that her lack of Irish rendered her unqualified for the job.

Dealing directly with the more controversial issue, of whether Miss Dunbar Harrison was a suitable appointment in an overwhelmingly Catholic county, he said, 'As regards the question of her religion it depended on what the duties and functions of a librarian are. If it was an educational matter, it must be faced frankly as a denominational one ... Catholic schools had Catholic teachers. It would not be fair to compel the Catholic community, who held conscientious views on matters like this, to put them aside for any consideration ... Fianna Fáil maintained that every person in the country, no matter of what religious faith, was entitled to a share of public appointments.'[11]

Mr de Valera concluded that the situation in the South was very different to that in the North. 'We do not intend to follow in their footsteps down here,' he said, 'and to ignore the rights of minorities. We stand for seeing that minorities get their rights, and there are ways of seeing they get them rather than by violating the opinions of a conscientious Catholic majority.' This seems to be a clear case of de Valera having his cake and eating it too; claiming to oppose discrimination in theory yet endorsing it in this particular instance.

'The Mayo damp squib'

The Cumann na nGaedheal newspaper, *An Reult* [*The Star*], unsurprisingly took a different stance. Under the headline 'The Mayo Damp Squib' it declared that 'the controversy which it has been sought to work up over the Mayo library appointment shows signs of dying of inanition … the fogs of propaganda created around the Mayo situation by not altogether disinterested champions of "Faith and Fatherland" … please spare us the crocodile tears … it appears to be pretty evident that the Mayo County Council has gone down unwept, unhonoured and unsung … outside of the limited ranks of the anti-government forces not a solitary cry appears to have been heard locally.'[12] This statement contains a large amount of wishful thinking. It was as if, having stood up to the pressure and faced down the original resistance, the Cumann na nGaedheal government hoped that the opponents of Miss Dunbar Harrison's appointment would simply fade away. If this was indeed their hope, they were soon to be disappointed.

Seán Ruane, a Cumann na nGaedheal councillor from Kiltimagh, wrote to President Cosgrave in December, warning him that there was talk of the establishment of a 'Catholic Centre Party' and that the prospect of the suppression of Mayo County Council 'is giving more pleasure than I like to some people not quite in love with the government or the government party.' Nevertheless, he continued, 'I have definitely made up my mind to sink or swim with Cumann na nGaedheal.'[13]

Seán Ruane was true to his word. Despite his private misgivings he had spoken strongly in favour of the party line at the special meeting of Mayo County Council. Cumann na nGaedheal needed more of this sort of party loyalty. The talk of a Catholic Centre Party seems to have been just that, talk. However, there was still some fight left in the council. Despite the dissolution, some of the councillors decided to ignore the government's action and called a meeting which was held in the council chamber of Castlebar courthouse. At this stage they had no legal right to be there. Pat Higgins, T.S. Moclair and John Morahan were the main movers. Sixteen councillors, by now ex-members of the council, turned up on Saturday, 10 January 1931. Following a discussion they opted to hold the meeting in private. As the *Mayo News* reported, 'It was decided to hold the proceedings in committee, much to the disgust of the gallery, some of whom were inclined to grumble.'[14] This unofficial meeting passed a number of motions:

1) Refusing to recognise the dissolution.
2) Demanding of the Minister for Local Government not to levy a rate for the Mayo library service on the grounds that it would be a waste as the service could not function.
3) Expressing thanks to Leitrim County Council and others for their support.
4) Requesting members of all committees appointed by the council to decline to recognise the action of the Department of Local Government and ask them not to operate under the order of the nominated commissioner, Mr Bartley.
5) Calling upon the nine TDs representing the county to oppose the government in the Dáil.

Mayo's mutiny was attracting attention elsewhere in Ireland. *The Irish Times* reported that Carlow County Council held a special meeting on 16 January 1931 and supported the attitude taken by Mayo. A motion was passed, 'that we take the opportunity of heartily congratulating our brother councillors in Mayo on the decided action they have taken in the cause of justice and liberty. We consider that it is high time that action of this kind was taken in Ireland to prove to the government, or any would-be oppressors, that they cannot over-ride the will of the people. Mayo councillors have set an example which could with credit be emulated in every county in the Free State.'[15]

'The conscience of the ninety-nine per cent'

The unrest soon spread as far as the capital. The *Irish Independent* reported that Councillor Fogarty of Dublin County Council had proposed a resolution expressing support for their counterparts in Mayo in rejecting the appointment of Miss Dunbar Harrison. The resolution also called on the government to introduce legislation that would restore the power of the council to appoint officials to local bodies. The council voted in favour of the resolution by twelve votes to eight. The chairman, J.J. Shiel, supported the motion because according to him the action of the Mayo representatives was the action of men discharging their duty as a matter of conscience and trust, representing as they were 99 per cent of the people of Mayo. A librarian was in charge of the education of the young and was an influence on the old, and 'with modern literature taking the turn it was taking, it was of extreme importance that there should be supervision of literature according to the conscience of the 99 per cent.'[16]

Not every attempt at rallying support for Mayo County Council proved successful. A motion condemning the government's action in usurping the power of the local authorities and congratulating Mayo on resisting this tyranny was 'ruled out of order at a meeting of the Donegal County Council on the grounds that it was irrelevant.'[17]

In late January a small article appeared in *The Connaught Telegraph* written by Miss Dunbar Harrison herself. It was entitled 'Library Notes'.

> Public libraries have what the people want. The people may not know, perhaps. It is their right to know. It is someone's business to tell them.
>
> This feature has been started because we, who are responsible for the progress of the Mayo County library, have recognised our obligation to tell the people of Mayo that we have what they want.
>
> The Mayo library scheme is something everyone is justly proud of, and, in the four years since its inception, it has striven to cater for the needs of the reading public within the county. But these are days of progression; this is an age in which to stand still means to be passed by and forgotten.

The world of today has no use for people or institutions that are not fully alive to the possibilities of the hour, and so we seek for the co-operation of every friend of books within the county, so that the library may not only hold its own, but press forward to a wider usefulness.

The library has been called the 'People's University', and its doors are open to all; it is up to the people to see that they make the fullest possible use of this great opportunity of free education. To the readers who are already enjoying the facilities of our service, we send this message: 'Go and tell others'; and to any who have not yet discovered the treasures of book-lore, we issue a cordial welcome: 'Come and see'.

There are over 130 centres working throughout the county, where the books are being distributed by local librarians. If anyone is in any doubt about the location of his or her nearest library, we shall be glad to give all details.

Apart from a very large selection of popular fiction, we have special sections in agriculture, Irish history and biography, books of local interest, Irish language and literature; and we cater specially for juvenile readers who are always most welcome in the ranks of library supporters.

We hope very shortly to be able to send round lists of some of the more recent additions to our special sections, as well as a list of Irish historical novels and novels by Catholic authors; these lists will be on view in the local centres, and readers may send in requests for any books they would like to have included in subsequent consignments.

We would also like to remind student borrowers of the facilities afforded by the Central Library for Students in Merrion Square, which supplies books over 6 shillings which are not easily obtained elsewhere. Forms of application may be held from the County Librarian.

In conclusion, the Librarian would welcome notes of constructive criticism on books which readers have enjoyed and would like to re-commend to others. New books as added will be briefly reviewed here.

With her references to 'novels by Catholic authors' and to 'books of Irish language and interest', it is clear that Miss Dunbar Harrison was aware of the scale of the opposition to her appointment and she was indicating her willingness to take account of the fears and suspicions of those opponents. Whether these adversaries were prepared to accept any compromise was a different matter.

Chapter 10

'Flappers who could not cook their father's dinner'

The county that most closely followed Mayo's lead was Leitrim. One of the five county librarian vacancies mentioned by President Cosgrave in his Dáil statement on 11 December had been situated in Leitrim. Miss Kathleen White had finished fifth in rank at the set of interviews that had been held to fill these vacancies. Like Miss Dunbar Harrison, Miss White was judged to have inadequate Irish but the selection board deemed her successful at the overall interview. After Miss Dunbar Harrison chose Mayo, the only vacancy left for Miss White was lovely Leitrim.

The provision of a county-wide library service had been a contentious issue in Leitrim. In 1930, following two abortive discussions, the County Council had decided by a narrow majority to adopt the Public Libraries Act for Leitrim. The main opposition to the act had come from Fianna Fáil and independent members of the council, and the proposal had only scraped through by thirteen votes to eleven.[1] At a further meeting a rescinding motion was narrowly defeated. It was agreed that a library committee should be formed and Ballinamore was selected as the main centre for the proposed service. As a local paper put it, there the matter rested until the Mayo controversy erupted. 'Beyond that,' wrote *The Anglo-Celt*, 'no step was taken save to ask the Appointments Commission to advertise for a librarian, with the proviso that Leitrim candidates would get the right of preference in selecting one for the post. The commissioners recommended a Miss White (stated … to be the daughter of the ex-Crown Solicitor of Queen's County [Laois], and now the county registrar) and the matter was referred back to know if any Leitrim candidates applied and the answer was received which was considered evasive, as it stated that in making the choice the commissioners selected those with library training.'[2]

With the full knowledge of what had taken place in Mayo, a special meeting of Leitrim County Council was held in Carrick-on-Shannon on Monday, 5 January 1931, to discuss the formation of a library committee and the appointment of a county librarian. On the agenda also was a motion to 'rescind the former resolution passed adopting the Public Libraries Act and that no rate be struck for the same in our estimate for 1931-32.'[3]

'It was well known,' continued *The Anglo-Celt*, 'that practically from the outset the general public were against the adoption of the act in the county, and it was, therefore, no surprise to find the country people coming in large numbers to town on Saturday and in reminiscent fashion of the old days, to see the Jamestown and Gowel fife and drum bands marching at their head and playing to the county courthouse doors where loud cheers were raised and their opposition voiced.'[4]

In a similar fashion to the special meeting in Mayo, the local population seemed to treat it as a form of free entertainment. Inside, the chamber was 'packed to suffocation, and when any member prior, and subsequent to the debate, made any remark that was popular, cheers were raised.'[5] Councillor Dominick Duignan, an auctioneer from Kiltycarney, who headed the farmers' deputation, revealed that the last time he had spoken against the act it had been threatened that he would be thrown through the window, but he was there to tell them, on behalf of the large gathering of representative ratepayers present, that they did not want the library.[6] They were not against education or learning in County Leitrim and as a people, if given a chance, they were well able to hold their own with anyone. He objected that 'flappers who could not cook their father's dinner were asked to read *The Sorrows of Satan*.'[7] Not only that, if the people should have the right to make the appointment of librarian and they could give it to a native of the county and thus keep one from emigrating, then there might be something in the proposed library service. He wondered what the teachers who advocated the library thought, when out of a population of 50,000 one could not be found to fill this post.

'Dick [Mulcahy] will send down one,' suggested a heckler.

'A stench in the nostrils of the people'

Councillor Duignan asked if the county that had produced Seán McDermott, 'whose blood splashed the walls for the freedom of the country', was not entitled to appoint one of their own? He proposed that they do the same as gallant Mayo, the home of John McHale and Michael Davitt, and he appealed to them not to take the insult offered to the county of Brian Oge and Seán McDermott, but fling it back by refusing to appoint the selection of the Bagwells and the Cromwells.[8]

Councillor Andrew Mooney from Drumshambo stated that he had been one of the strongest advocates of the library but he had found that the people did not want it. Recent events had made the successful working of the library impossible. They would need to be careful and not land themselves where Mayo is. Things had happened, he said, that had made the question of the libraries a 'stench in the nostrils of the people.'[9]

Mr Pettit, solicitor to the council, was invited to speak. He said that there was nothing to compel them to adopt the Public Libraries Act if they did not want it.

'I take it we will not be liable?' Councillor John Reilly asked.

'I won't tell you that,' replied Mr Pettit. 'I am not so certain.'

'We don't oppose the librarian. We are against the whole act,' pointed out Councillor Creamer.[10]

The county secretary maintained that in the rate estimates for the current year the rate for the library had already been levied and collected. Councillor Reilly said that in that case, as far as he could see, they were liable. That finished the whole business. They would have to pay the librarian. Councillor Reilly was the only speaker in favour of the act. As the *Evening Herald* put it, Councillor Reilly had, 'when the matter was first raised voted against it, on the next occasion voted for it, and on the last occasion did not vote at all.'[11]

Councillor Michael McGrath seconded the motion to rescind Leitrim's adoption of the Public Libraries Act. He was adamant that no matter what they did there that day, let them not be like shivering mice and in no way afraid of the Appointments Commission. The chairman stated that he believed the council would be abolished, as had happened in Mayo, and they should be prepared to deal with that.

'And we are responsible for the lady's pay?' he asked the solicitor.

'You are up against that,' Mr Pettit conceded.[12]

Councillor Pat Kilkenny asserted that he had been against the adoption of the act from the beginning. He went on to congratulate Andrew Mooney. He had never felt so proud as when he saw Mr Mooney and his party come into the ranks of Fianna Fáil.

'I have not gone one step into your party,' replied Mooney.

'Indeed you have,' Councillor Kilkenny asserted.

'You have,' Councillor Creamer added, 'and we will make an archangel of you.'[13]

Councillor Ben Maguire asked what difference was there between Leitrim's position and that of Mayo? They had adopted the Public Libraries Act and asked the Appointments Commission to make a recommendation as to the person to be appointed librarian. The Mayo County Council were wiped out, and he could not see any difference between Mr Mooney's advocacy of the adoption of the library and his present opposition. The Appointments Commission had a monopoly over the public bodies.[14]

'The hind legs of a cow'
Councillor Higgins declared that Councillor Mooney's procedure was 'as straight as the hind legs of a cow.'

'Mr Higgins is playing to the gallery,' replied Councillor Mooney. 'I never play to the gallery.'

Councillor Reilly warned the meeting that the same fate would befall them as had happened in Mayo. The motion was carried with only Councillor Reilly dissenting.

'A great landslide,' declared Councillor McGowan.

A motion was then proposed congratulating Mayo County Council on the stand it took and condemning the Department of Local Government for abolishing it.

'Someone will be congratulating us after this,' Councillor Travers predicted to an outburst of laughter from the gallery.

'The west's awake,' announced Councillor Connolly. 'I support the resolution and I say it would be a lack on our part if we did not adopt it.'

Councillor Reilly said that he had always understood Mayo County Council to be able to mind its own business and there was no need for such a resolution.[15] Councillor Connolly went on to maintain that the case of Mayo might be theirs tomorrow and he was glad to see Mayo, the founder of greater agitations, starting an agitation against something that was certainly very doubtful. The resolution was passed and the discussion ended. The bands then struck up outside.[16]

The government moved quickly to take steps to quell the rebellion in Leitrim, proving just as resolute as they had been in the Mayo instance. Within weeks the *Leitrim Observer* reported, 'What is understood to be an ultimatum has been received from the Local Government Department, and intense interest is centred in the approaching duel between the Breffni County Council and the department.'[17]

'Each member of the Leitrim County Council,' wrote the *Irish Independent*, 'had been directed by telegram to attend a special meeting of the council to consider a communication of a peremptory nature from the Local Government Department, directing them it is understood, to put the Public Libraries Act into force and proceed with the appointment of a librarian.'[18]

There were animated scenes at the special meeting held on Saturday, 24 January. The full text of a letter from the Local Government Department, which was signed by E.P. McCarron, was read into the minutes. The councillors were reminded that they had already levied a rate for the library service so they could not rescind the Public Libraries Act for the county. They were also told that they had no option but to accept the recommendation of the Local Appointments Commission.

At the meeting Councillor McGrath sounded almost nostalgic for the days of yore. He stated that, 'In the days of the English, county councils had all powers in their hands. They were now like a lot of children going to school. They could not make a bog road for the accommodation of farmers.'

'The cleaning of the courthouse'
Councillor Mooney suggested that perhaps Miss White could be appointed librarian and subsequently dismissed a few months later. 'You could give her the cleaning of the courthouse,' Councillor Creamer proposed.[19]

The chairman, Michael Carter, told the meeting that he believed that if the council was dissolved the commissioner would then appoint a librarian.[20] This was perhaps the crux of the matter. Whatever they decided, Miss White was destined to become librarian as had happened with Miss Dunbar Harrison in Mayo. As Councillor P. Reynolds put it, 'All that has to be done on this matter is very simple, as we have debated the subject from every angle for over a year. That letter leaves us no option but to appoint a librarian and I propose that she be appointed.'

'Dances and night-walking'
Councillor Mooney said that 'it had been alleged against him that

he was more or less responsible for getting the council into the present situation.'

Councillor Connolly loudly added, 'You have led us into this corner, and get us out of it.' There was much laughter from the gallery. Councillor Mooney had been the original mover of the motion to adopt the Public Libraries Act.

As *The Anglo-Celt* reported at the time, 'In urging his motion he said there was no life in the country.'

To which Councillor Pye responded, 'There are any amount of dances.'

'If there were less dances and night-walking it would be better,' Councillor Mooney insisted.[21]

The Leitrim rebellion collapsed in the face of such determination, though not without a long debate and a certain amount of recrimination. As the *Leitrim Observer* put it, 'The threat of a commissioner had a subduing effect' though there were 'allegations about "corkscrews", "turncoats" and "twisters".'[22]

After a four-hour discussion the council voted, by fourteen votes to seven, to re-adopt the Public Libraries Act and appoint Miss Kathleen White as librarian. Six councillors, including Councillor Andrew Mooney, refused to vote one way or the other. The decision met with a mixed reaction. There were cheers and counter cheers from the public gallery.[23]

Leitrim County Council's short-lived revolt was perhaps inspired by the actions of Mayo County Council, but the uprising soon petered out on seeing how resolute central government had proved to be in the Mayo case. Leitrim County Council had previously been dissolved in 1923 so perhaps this too had an influence on their decision in this instance.

As is evident from Kathleen White's experience in Leitrim, the lack of spoken Irish was little more than a pretext to reject Miss Dunbar Harrison. Miss White had been placed behind Miss Dunbar Harrison by the selection board and she also did not have Irish. In all the debates in Leitrim this hardly came up at all. Although Miss White was met with a certain initial degree of distrust in the county due to her being an outsider, the level of hostility shown to her was much, much less than the outright hostility expressed towards Miss Dunbar Harrison in Mayo.

Chapter 11

'It was not a sectarian issue because, first of all, the Catholic church is not a sect'

As is evident from the Leitrim incident, many councillors opposed the introduction of a public library service as it would have to be funded from rates and would be a drain on scarce resources. Many members of the clergy distrusted libraries on the more general grounds that they were a conduit to the outside world, with the possibility of being an evil influence. The clergy saw it as their duty to serve on library committees to exercise some control over these new establishments. The Lenten letter of Archbishop Gilmartin of Tuam from 1931 is a good example of the typical attitude of the Catholic hierarchy towards the outside world:

> The modern world is teeming with all kinds of printed matter, books, more especially novels, reviews, magazines, papers – a few of them good, some of them indifferent, some of them positively immoral, many of them anti-Christian, and many of them illustrated with indecent pictures.
>
> Now we all know that the mind is formed by what it feeds upon. Hence you are invited to support the Catholic Truth Society which supplies wholesome and interesting reading matter and publishes catalogues of books that, speaking generally, it is safe to read.
>
> You are also exhorted to support and read our Irish papers, especially our splendid Catholic weeklies and to keep out of your homes that section of the foreign press, particularly the Sunday foreign press, which specialises in parading the crimes, the scandals, the filth and the irreligion of the world.

The world of books and newspapers was believed to be a wild and dangerous place that needed to be supervised and controlled.

NAME and SURNAME.	RELATION to Head of Family.	RELIGIOUS PROFESSION.	EDUCATION.	AGE (last Birthday) and SEX.	RANK, PROFESSION, OR OCCUPATION.	PARTICULARS AS TO MARRIAGE.	WHERE BORN.	IRISH LANGUAGE.	If Deaf and Dumb; Dumb only; Blind; Imbecile or Idiot; or Lunatic.
				Males / Females					
John Walter Harrison	Head	Church of Ireland	Read & write	47	Warehouseman	Married	Co. Wicklow		—
Sarah Elizabeth Harrison	Wife	do	Read & write	47		— 23 yrs —	Co. Wicklow		
Aileen Letitia Harrison	niece	do	do	5		Single	Co. Dublin		
Joshua Mary Doyle	Servant	Roman Catholic	Read & write	29	Cook, domestic servant	Single	— —	Co. Wicklow	

This page from the 1911 Census shows that Aileen Letitia Harrison was brought up by her aunt's family. Her uncle, John Walter Harrison's occupation is given as 'Warehouseman'. (NAI)

THE MAYO LIBRARY APPOINTMENT.

NEW LIBRARIAN TO START NEXT WEEK.

Miss Letitia Elizabeth Dunbar-Harrison, the recently appointed Librarian for County Mayo, intends to take up her new duties next week.

Born in Dublin in 1906, Miss Dunbar-Harrison is the niece and adopted daughter of the late Mr. John Harrison, and of Mrs. Harrison, of 72 Palmerston road, Dublin. She was educated at Alexandra School, Dublin, where she obtained honours in the Junior Grade, Intermediate, and won the Jeannie Turpin Essay Prize and the Helen Prenter Prize in English Literature. She remained at Alexandra School from

Now known as Letitia Elizabeth Dunbar Harrison (some newspapers added a hyphen, some did not) she graduated from Trinity College, Dublin, in 1928.

Standard

AN ORGAN OF IRISH CATHOLIC OPINION

VOL. 3. No. 31.   SATURDAY, DECEMBER 13, 1930.   PRICE TWOPENCE

WILL THE CATHOLICS OF MAYO BE OVER-RULED

WILL MAYO CO. COUNCIL BE DISSOLVED ?	SPECIAL FEATURES THIS WEEK	EIGHT YEARS OF FASCIS REVIEWED
An Extraordinary Rumour of Compulsory Secularism	Daniel Corkery on Books ... 8 Christian Doctrine in Irish 9 Rosemary and Holly ... 10 Only the Milkman ... ... 11 Persons and Places ... ... 5 Literary Notes and Notions 8	Italy To-day—Revival of Religion Prosperity of the Nation Specially Written for "The Standard"

Opposition to Dunbar Harrison's appointment was particularly prevalent in the Catholic press.

GOVERNMENT AND MAYO LIBRARIANSHIP.

BRIEF INQUIRY INTO COUNTY COUNCIL'S ATTITUDE.

REPORT TO BE PRESENTED TO MR. MULCAHY TO-DAY.

FROM OUR SPECIAL REPRESENTATIVE.
CASTLEBAR, Wednesday.

FROM the Local Government inquiry into the conduct of affairs by the Mayo County Council, which was held here to-day, two facts emerge:

(1)—The County Council, generally speaking, has discharged its duties efficiently.

(2)—In ratifying the refusal of the Library Committee to appoint as County Librarian Miss Letitia Elizabeth Dunbar, B.A., T.C.D.—who was selected by the Local Appointments Commission—it has not acted in accordance with its obligations.

The result, I believe, will be the dissolution of the County Council, and the appointment of a Commissioner to administer the affairs of the county.

The Minister (Mr. Mulcahy) will receive the report of the Inspector to-morrow morning, and it is anticipated

The Government inquiry into the workings of Mayo County Council was a brisk affair; it lasted less than half-an-hour.

DISSOLUTION OF MAYO CO. COUNCIL.—An exclusive photograph of the new Commissioner, Mr. P. J. Bartley, in office at Castlebar.—"Evening Herald" Photo.

P.J. Bartley took over the running of Mayo County Council in January 1931. The newspapers were impressed with his businesslike attitude. 'It will be a half-holiday for the press today', he told them at the end of his first public meeting.

MAYO CO. COUNCIL DISSOLVED.—... r. P. J. Bartley (right), who took over .ne administration of the Co. Mayo affairs consequent to the dissolution of the Co. Council, photographed with officers of the Council. The Secretary, Mr. M, J. F...n, is seen in centre.—" Evening Herald " Photo.

Christina Keogh is seated front row second from the left, Tom Gay is the man standing at her shoulder, fourth from the left.

It wasn't all work at library conferences. This scenic location is Glengariff, County Cork.

Right: *The memory of Seán na Sagart as a folk-demon lived long with the people of Mayo.*

Below: *The two advertisements show clearly the change in emphasis of the Local Appointments Commission between February and May 1930 with regard to the county librarian vacancies. The crucial difference is that in the first one, knowledge of Irish was deemed essential; in the second one it was merely desirable.*

County Librarians, Mayo, Cavan, Carlow, Kilkenny, Leitrim.					Interview 4th April, 1930.	
General Education. 100	Professional Qualifications. 150	Practical Library Experience. 100	Special Experience. 150	Personality. 200	Irish. + or -	Total. 700
McLeod, Iona M. 65	100	45	45	120	+75/	375
Barron, Brigid. 75	40	40	40	150	+75/	345
Harrison, Letitia E.A. 80	0	50	40	150	-20/	320
White, Kathleen M. 50	0	50	80	100	-20/	280

County Librarians, Mayo, Leitrim, Cavan, Meath and Waterford.					Interview 12th July, 1930.	
MacNevin, Mary K. 100	0	100	150	180	+80%	530
Guise-Brown, Gerald E. 75	100	10	0	180	-10%	365
MacMurchadha, Fergus. 60	100	50	50	100	+75/	360
Burke, Ellen. 65	100	10	0	75	-40/	250

The State Papers include this document which shows the marks obtained by Letitia Dunbar Harrison and the other successful candidates. The marks of Ellen Burke are also shown. Miss Burke received 75 marks out of a possible 200 for 'Personality'. (NAI, D/Taoiseach S 2547B)

SURPRISE IN MAYO LIBRARY DISPUTE

MISS HARRISON TO RESIGN

AMICABLE SETTLEMENT AFTER MONTHS OF CONTROVERSY

CONTESTED APPOINTMENT

The fifteen months' old dispute between the Mayo Co. Council and the Dept. of Local Government in connection with the refusal of the Co. Council in October, 1930, to appoint Miss L. Dunbar Harrison as Co. Librarian, is about to be settled amicably, writes the Political Correspondent of the *Irish Independent.*

Miss Harrison, I understand, has decided to resign from the post, if she has not already actually done so. As she has very high qualifications as a librarian, she is, it appears, likely to secure an important appointment elsewhere. But with her in Mayo with regret, because during her time there, although the library scheme has not functioned as it might otherwise have, the kindly attitude of the people has touched her very much. The Library Committee was dissolved some time ago for failure to perform its duties, and two Inspectors of the

DUBLIN'S NEW GALLERY OF MODERN ART

The Dublin Corporation Lane Pictures Claim Committee paid a visit recently to the new Gallery of Modern Art and Civic Museum...

FROM IRELAND TO CEYLON
LEADERS AND NEW YEAR

IRISHMAN'S PLANS

CHICAGO'S NEW PROBLEM
GREAT CITY FACES BANKRUPTCY

FIRST EFFECTS OF BACON TARIFF

| IRISH PRICES' UPWARD BOUND | A WATERFORD FACTORY TO REOPEN? |

TRADERS' OPTIMISTIC VIEWS

NORTHERN IRELAND TO BENEFIT BY IMPOST

The drastic import duty on bacon, which virtually excludes products from countries outside the British Commonwealth, has, on the whole, received a warm welcome in the Saorstat.

While it is admitted that the first effect of the Government action will be an increase in home prices—there was a general rise yesterday—it is felt that the Saorstat industry has been provided with a splendid opportunity of improving its position, and that fortunes will benefit considerably.

Waterford Factory Hope

Opinion is held in Waterford that the tariff will result in the re-opening of a bacon factory there which was closed six months ago, chiefly because of foreign dumping.

THE WORLD'S NEWS   WEDNESDAY, *Irish Independent* JANUARY 6, 1932.   7

NEW POST FOR COUNTY MAYO LIBRARIAN

MISS HARRISON FOR DUBLIN

DEPARTMENT OF DEFENCE APPOINTMENT

SPECIAL INTERVIEW IN CITY

Our *Irish Independent* is to-day in a position to announce that Miss L. Dunbar Harrison has been appointed Librarian at the Department of Defence, Dublin.

A exclusive announcement of Miss Harrison's forthcoming resignation from the Co. Mayo Librarianship was made in the *Irish Independent* last Friday.

As it an extensive library at Military Headquarters, Parkgate St., and it was decided some time ago to appoint a Librarian to supervise it.

Not in the complications which necessitated the appointment of Miss Harrison in Co. Mayo she was, it appears, invited to apply for the post.

... was in Dublin for a special interview within the last few weeks, writes the Political Correspondent of the *Irish Independent.*

BARGAINS BY POST

NOVEL SCHEME BY THE "IRISH INDEPENDENT"

ENLISTING RADIO

TO MAKE SHOPPING EASIER

"Shopping from the armchair," is a slogan which may well be applied to the new scheme of combined Press and Radio advertising which the *Irish Independent*, with its centenary enterprise, will inaugurate in conjunction with the advertisers on Saturday next.

The chief attraction of the scheme is an arrangement whereby a special weekly broadcast from the Dublin and Cork stations will be given on each Friday night for the next six weeks.

A VIEW OF ROUNDWOOD RESERVOIR.

ROUNDING-UP INDIAN CONGRESS LEADERS

WATER WASTAGE IN DUBLIN

ENORMOUS INCREASE IN THE CONSUMPTION

CITY ENGINEER'S SERIOUS WARNING AND APPEAL TO THE CITIZENS

SUPPLIES MAY BE CURTAILE[D]

After a year of controversy, rumours began in the press that the crisis in Mayo was about to be resolved.

A post of Librarian on the salary scale £100-£25-£200 per annum, plus bonus, in the Department of Industry and Commerce is vacant. The person appointed to the post should have a knowledge of modern languages and have qualifications and experience in library work.

The Minister for ~~Industry and Commerce~~ *Defence* has proposed, and the Minister for Finance has concurred in the proposal, that this post should be filled by the appointment of Miss Letitia Dunbar, at present Librarian under a Local Authority. Miss Dunbar is a qualified and experienced Librarian and is the possessor of a University Honours Degree in modern languages. It is understood that, if offered the appointment, she is willing to accept it. She would enter the scale fixed for the post at a point equivalent to her present remuneration (£250 per annum inclusive).

The Minister for ~~Industry and Commerce~~ *Defence*, with the concurrence of the Minister for Finance, accordingly recommend to the Executive Council that Miss Dunbar should be appointed Librarian in the Department of ~~Industry and~~ *Defence* Commerce, and that the appointment should proceed as one to be made in the public interest under Section 3 "6 (2)" of the Civil Service Regulation (Amendment) Act, 1926.

ROINN AIRGID.

Mi na Nodlag, 1931.

As is clear from this memo date-stamped 22 December 1931, the government was more concerned with moving Letitia Dunbar Harrison, than with where she would end up. The original intention seems to have been to find her a post with the Department of Industry and Commerce.
(NAI, D/Taioseach S 2547B)

Rev. Crawford was a Methodist Minister based in Castlebar at the time Letitia Dunbar Harrison was appointed county librarian. The couple married in June 1932. (Rev. Robin Roddie, Wesley Historical Society of Ireland)

The Rev. R. C. Crawford.

Group of delegates who attended the conference organised by the Library Association of Ireland, held at University College, Cork, from 3 to 9 June 1933. About one third of the delegates are female, reflecting the gender balance of the profession at the time. Librarianship was seen as a suitable job for a woman.

The controversy over the appointment of librarians was linked in the minds of many councillors and clergy to the touchy subject of how medical officers should be appointed in the local authorities. Medical appointments were seen as especially sensitive on political and religious grounds. Contraception and abortion were illegal in Ireland yet the Anglican church's Lambeth Conference had debated such issues as birth control and given approval to the use of contraceptives in certain cases. The Catholic church wanted, if not control, at least a strong say into how such posts were filled.

As the *Catholic Bulletin* put it, 'More is needed than a librarian described as being Catholic. Not every Catholic, so called, can be admitted to such public duties towards a Catholic people. There are not a few persons styled Catholic, in this Carnegie library movement, who cannot but be regarded as very doubtfully fitted for such duties.

'They had eulogies and appreciations of such unworthy writers as Joyce, Moore, O'Flaherty, O'Casey, not to mention those obscene English pen-men, D.H. Lawrence and his associates, always ready for the subsidised weekly journal of Messers H. Plunkett, G.W. Russell and Lennox Robinson. Only a thoroughly educated Catholic man or woman, loyal and energetic in the cause of Catholic action, can be deemed fit for the highly responsible and influential post of county librarian.'[1]

In the early days of the New Year, resistance to the county librarian spread throughout Mayo. The *Western People* reported that the Ballina library sub-committee had dissolved itself in protest to Miss Dunbar Harrison's employment. The chairman, Rev. Denis O'Connor, stated, 'It was not a sectarian issue because first of all the Catholic church was not a sect. It was not sectarianism but a stand on Catholic principles.'[2]

A correspondent for the *Irish Independent* described the scene in the Ballina library room where some of the voluntary helpers 'were busily engaged in packing the books into boxes for the purpose of dispatch to Castlebar.'[3] The *Connacht Tribune* predicted the demise of the libraries in Mayo. 'Though opinion on the matter may be divided,' it wrote, 'there is one outcome apparent even at this early stage, and that is that Mayo county library will become a dead letter.'[4]

'The blunt truth'

The *Mayo News* printed an article from the *Irish World*, a New York paper. 'Every anti-Irish institution in Britain and this country,' it wrote, 'is beginning to concentrate on what has come to be known as the Dunbar case.' The *Irish World* went on to accuse Richard Mulcahy of giving ammunition to the anti-Irish the world over:

> His action will be represented as a case where the local public body had to be abolished in order to get a Protestant appointed … the Junta will give colour to the lie that only the greatest force will secure an appointment in the 'Free' State for a Protestant. The facts are almost absurdly the other way … In the Free State area where the Catholics form 93 per cent of the population and Protestants 7 per cent, the Protestants have 15 per cent of the total state positions.
>
> … the Junta, in their preparations to suppress Mayo County Council, are giving face to a shameful lie – that Protestants are not getting a fair show in the Free State … The Junta will not protest against things like that which are daily occurring in the six counties. They must act so as to give the impression that Irish public bodies have to be suppressed before they will give fair play to a minority which in blunt truth is not only fairly treated at this moment but is almost absurdly pampered.[5]

'Dancing to the tune of The Irish Times'

Irish-American newspapers were, unsurprisingly, critical of the suppression of Mayo County Council. The *Roscommon Herald* quoted an unnamed 'Chicago Catholic organ' as accusing the government of 'dancing to the tune of *The Irish Times* and the "occult influence" of the imperialist minority in the Free State.'[6]

The *Catholic Times* in England held similar views. 'Nobody believes, of course,' it wrote, 'that the matter can end here, that the Mayo County Council has vainly sacrificed itself. The situation will arise again in an aggravated form in Kerry, or Donegal or Tipperary … [The situation] has impressed upon dependable Catholics the great need of Catholic action … as public men they have a greater duty to their religion, than the recital of the "Angelus", cap in hand, on the public street of some country town. Catholic action has to do for them and the coming generation what, in the field of politics their nationalist masters did for them and their country. It has to give expression to the Catholic mind of the people.'[7]

What the Catholic mind of the people demanded and Catholic action entailed in this case, was the boycotting of the library service. As the month of January wore on and the political debate continued at home and abroad, this boycott spread across the county. 'Meanwhile the books are coming back to the library by the hundred,' wrote the *Mayo News*, 'but whether they will ever again go out is not so certain. Train, bus and lorry bring the familiar boxes, and the approaches to the library door are constantly filled, but no books are allowed out at the moment, and in any case there are no applications for them.'[8] It was clear that the Catholic clergy were the main movers, if not the instigators, of the boycott.

'Charlestown's answer'

The *Western People* reported that 'an emphatic request to have all the Carnegie library books dispatched to Castlebar within this week was made at all the masses in Charlestown on Sunday last.' Fr Denis Gildea cited the fourth commandment as the basis for the opposition. Governments exist for the furtherance of the good of the community. Subjects have rights as well as duties. The common good, the welfare of the people of County Mayo, demands that if a duly qualified Catholic librarian is available, such a one should be put in charge in preference to a Protestant. The imposition of a

Protestant lady showed an overweening contempt for the welfare of the community and must be resisted. And that resistance would take the form of returning, at once, all books circulating in Charlestown parish to Miss Letitia Dunbar Harrison.[9]

Meanwhile, the Pioneer Hall Committee of Castlebar's lending library refused to accept any more books from the central library and requested to have the books removed. The *Irish Independent* reported that 'Ballinrobe library committee has closed and returned all the books to Castlebar as a protest against the appointment of the new librarian. The library had an average of fifty readers.'[10]

By the end of January the government's hopes that the crisis in Mayo would abate once the rebellion of the council was faced down, had proved false. Under the heading 'Books Coming Home', the *Western People* reported, 'South and west Mayo are now following the lead given by the library committee in Ballina in sending back all Carnegie library books to Castlebar as a protest against the appointment of Miss Dunbar. In fact by the end of this week all books from west Mayo will be returned, with the intimation, written occasionally in Irish, that the centres are abolished and will not again be erected until the Mayo librarian suits the people of Mayo.

'South Mayo centres are gathering up their scattered books as fast as possible, and within a month, it will be a rare bird of a book that has not come home to roost. Of course, long ago it was easy to see that such would be the case; the logical result of the controversy will be that the Mayo library books will remain on their shelves gathering dust.'[11]

The *Irish Independent* managed to get a statement from Miss Dunbar Harrison. On 26 February she told the paper 'that stabilised conditions had not yet been reached, the opposition to her appointment having resulted in the closing down of a large number of branches in rural and town areas and the books having been returned to the central repository.' There had been some falling off in the patrons of the central library and the branch in Castlebar, she said, which was somewhat of an understatement. Yet she remained positive. She also stated that 'arrangements had been made for her to visit all the districts with a view to re-establishing the discontinued centres and the opening of new ones. The people of all classes were kind and courteous, and she was confident that she would be happy among them. The people were wonderful readers and had set great value on the books.'[12] She insisted that she would fulfil the conditions regarding Irish within the allotted time.

The *Catholic Bulletin* was keeping a close eye on the situation. 'Miss Dunbar,' it wrote, 'is also eloquent on her supporters and advisers in the Castlebar area. Beyond the types represented by the purchased degree holders of TCD and the devotees of mixed education as represented by the defunct Queen's Colleges of Sir Robert Peel, who are they?'[13]

By June, the *Catholic Bulletin* had assured its readers that of the 130 or so library centres that had been active in Mayo in December 1930, less than five of them were in use by May 1931. They were exceedingly proud of what they saw as an example of Catholic action. It was evident that the Mayo library service was being boycotted. As one historian put it, 'It was clear that if Mayo did not have a Catholic librarian, it would have no library at all.'[14]

Not just as a strategy but even as a word, boycotting had a strong resonance in Mayo. It was here that it had originated during the Land League's campaign in the 1880s. A form of extreme social ostracisation, not everyone was in favour of it as a policy. In his book *Boycott*, Charles Boycott (not a disinterested commentator) describes it as 'a most unpleasant, much feared and widely used social weapon in Ireland, and, before long, in the world.'[15] What happened with the library service in Mayo in the early months of 1931 may have been on the milder side of the scale compared, for instance, to the Fethard-on-Sea boycott, but it cannot have been a pleasant experience for a young librarian.[16] As Archdeacon Fallon put it, 'The people of Castlebar have shown no antagonism to Miss Harrison personally. They have shown every mark of courtesy to her as a refined, cultured young lady.' However, he went on to say, 'The action of the County Council in refusing to appoint her, and the action of the people of Mayo in returning all the books, is proof enough to show that they will not have her services as a librarian.'

To make matters worse for the government the difficulties had begun to spread to other areas of Commissioner Bartley's work in the county. The *Western People* headlined a report, 'Mayo Vocational Committee – Only One Member Attends'. It wrote, 'Very Rev. Canon McHugh, PP, VF, Claremorris, was the only member of Mayo Vocational Educational Committee who answered the summons for the monthly meeting on Tuesday, 29 January.'[17] This was the only County Council committee that had not been abolished, though the members of the council selected to represent it had been removed by the commissioner, leaving it to function with a mere handful of clergymen and representatives from the urban councils. However, it seemed that these too had joined in the protest and were refusing to co-operate with Commissioner Bartley's new regime.

The people of Mayo seemed determined to show that they could survive without a library service. And now that the dispute was spreading, a resolution to the crisis seemed as far away as ever. In the face of the stubbornness of the people, the government's strategy was in tatters.

Chapter 12

'Gore-grimed tomahawks'

Realising at last that they were in for a long battle, the Cumann na nGaedheal government decided to concentrate their efforts on the Catholic hierarchy. If they could come up with a solution that would satisfy the bishops, it was felt that they would be able to sway public opinion in Mayo and that Fianna Fáil's opposition would then wither away. The conservative Catholic press's response to the Mayo controversy was frenzied. In January 1931, the *Catholic Bulletin* issued an editorial headlined 'The Mayo Librarianship Thundered'.

'Whether her name be Miss Dunbar or Miss Harrison or something else,' it wrote, 'she is in no sense personally in question. What is in question arises entirely because of the character and aims of her college and university, of Trinity College Dublin ... Trinity College – a tainted source ... were Miss Dunbar far more qualified than she is thought to be by the Local Appointments Commissioners the basic obstacles to her appointment as county librarian for Mayo would be intensified instead of being diminished ... [This] applies in full measure even to that essential knowledge of Irish which she does not possess.'[1]

As was its approach in most circumstances, the *Catholic Bulletin* regarded Trinity College as the villain of the piece, crediting it with enormous power and influence within the Free State.

A month later and the *Catholic Bulletin* had not calmed down. Its February lead editorial, headlined 'Well Done Mayo', directed most of its ire at the Minister for Local Government. It referred to Richard Mulcahy as 'a politico-military bully ... indulging his splenetic spirit of bullying despotism ... The mind of Mayo has from the start been set solidly on the vital Catholic position in this question.'

The journal was vehemently against the Local Appointments system. 'Any and every County Council in Ireland,' it wrote, 'is as intelligent and is a good deal more honest than this thoroughly unworthy monopoly system. It was devised and set up in that nest of ascendancy men and their tame toadies, the Local Government Board.'[2]

The Catholic Standard was only slightly more moderate in its opinions. It asked if the dissolution of Mayo Council meant 'that a Catholic people's demand, expressed by its authoritative representatives, to possess a Catholic system of education, may be followed by a suppression of its liberties?' In an editorial headlined 'Naked Secularism', *The Catholic Standard* was critical of the reasons given by Fianna Fáil for rejecting Miss Dunbar Harrison. 'These secularists,' it argued, 'opposed Miss Dunbar's appointment on the linguistic grounds.'[3] They were castigated for doing the 'right' thing but for the 'wrong' reason.

The Nation responded to criticisms in the Catholic press of the republican stance of Fianna Fáil's Mayo TDs, Mr Ruttledge and Mr Walsh. 'In our view,' it wrote, 'the issue is simply one of justice. The Fianna Fáil deputies refused to accept Miss Dunbar because she was not qualified in this essential particular but they had the manliness and courage to disassociate themselves from the prejudices which found expression at the library committee meeting.'[4]

In January 1931 the other radical periodical *The Catholic Mind* (incorporating *The Catholic Pictorial*) carried an editorial headlined 'The Mayo Library Case'. The editorial stated that 'tolerance is not in itself a virtue ... We regret exceedingly that the Mayo library committee did not take its stand boldly on the Catholic issue. There was no mention of that issue in the resolution they passed. It was a nationalist resolution.'[5]

There was intense competition between the Catholic papers over which of them could be the most outspoken. This led to some inter-journal sniping. *The Catholic Mind* attacked *The Catholic Standard* for not being sufficiently strong-minded. 'We detest hysteria; "naked secularism" and that sort of stuff,' it wrote. 'We do not mind good, honest slaughter. Gore-grimed tomahawks do not disturb us. In fact we delight in the profusion of scalps which adorns our wigwam.'[6]

Richard Mulcahy, as Minister for Local Government, still held a firm line publicly. President Cosgrave gave him strong backing, as did the cabinet. However, in private they were attempting to reach a compromise. Informal feelers were sent out to gauge the attitude of the Catholic hierarchy. The matter was complicated somewhat in that there were already difficulties over the appointment of dispensary doctors, an issue generally perceived to be even more sensitive.

Sir Joseph Glynn was put forward as the Cumann na nGaedheal government's emissary to the Catholic hierarchy, a sort of semi-official ambassador. Joseph Glynn was born in 1869 and educated at Blackrock College. He studied law at UCD and was also the first chairman of the National Health Insurance Commission 1912-1940. A Dublin businessman, he was heavily involved in charitable works. For a time he was president of the St Vincent de Paul Society and the Catholic Truth Society. In 1913 he was elected president of Blackrock College's Past Pupils' Union. He was honoured with a papal knighthood. In later life he wrote a biography of Matt Talbot. In short he was the kind of eminently respectable Catholic that could act as a go-between for the government and the hierarchy.

The intention was for Joseph Glynn to meet with the Archbishop of Tuam, Thomas Gilmartin, the senior member of the hierarchy in the area. The County of Mayo consisted of a number of dioceses of which Tuam was the most important. As early as 8 February, Sir Joseph met up with the vicar general of the Tuam archdiocese, Monsignor Walsh, who was also president of St Jarlaths in Tuam, for exploratory discussions. President Cosgrave had given him, 'for transmission to His Grace the archbishop of Tuam', the Local Appointments Commissioners' report on the Mayo librarian appointment. He passed these details on to Monsignor Walsh.

To modern ears there is a certain careful tone to President Cosgrave's attitude to the bishops. President Cosgrave may have been the leader of a sovereign government, but he was very wary of offending the Catholic hierarchy in any way. At times he almost seemed to be going cap-in-hand to them, as this note from President Cosgrave to Archbishop Gilmartin shows, 'I am very grateful for Your Grace's help in our effort to prevent a situation arising in which the good relations happily existing between the church and state may be endangered. We are most anxious to avoid any such development.'[7]

The government explored a number of possible solutions to the general librarian problem rather than the specific case. But the hierarchy was intractably adamant; they would not tolerate Miss Dunbar Harrison being left in the post in Mayo. In many ways the bishops were more relaxed about the dispute, secure in the knowledge that they held the stronger hand. Archbishop Gilmartin remarked to Sir Joseph Glynn 'that it was inevitable in a "neutral state" that the church might put forward a case to which the government of the state would be unable to accede.'[8] President Cosgrave felt that some of the criticism was unwarranted. There is a hurt tone to the Cumann na nGaedheal government's remarks, as in this memo circulated to the Catholic hierarchy:

> In general it is unfair, and not conducive to good government, to order, or the interests of the church, for the bishops to attack the government on every occasion where they may differ from them, without first having laid their views before the government, and heard the government's reply. The bishops may have been misinformed, they may not see that their demands are impracticable, that they are asking what the government cannot grant … Friendly co-operation between church and state will smooth away much misunderstanding and make peaceful government easier. The bishops will find the government most

accommodating, willing and even anxious to meet their Lordship's wishes as far as it is possible.[9]

Evidently, Cumann na nGaedheal had been so long in power that they identified any attack on their party or their policies as an attack on the state itself, an occupational hazard of any party in power too long.

In general we suggest that the bishops make representations to the government directly when they have cause of complaint or any suggestions to offer. It is embarrassing to the government to learn the bishops' views through a condemnatory pastoral letter or a chance conversation between a bishop and a minister. The government feels it has a grievance here.[10]

The government's immediate short-term aim had been to persuade the local bishops not to mention the Mayo controversy in their Lenten letters. The reason they gave was that it would be more difficult to reach a compromise if the bishops went public with their opposition as they [the government] could not be seen to be buckling under clerical pressure. In this convoluted and slightly cynical argument they were not successful. Archbishop Gilmartin referred directly to the Mayo controversy in his message to his flock. 'Such being the influence of printed matter,' he said, 'and the difficulty of discriminating between what is good and what is bad, it is gratifying to see how the representatives of our Catholic people are unwilling to subsidise libraries not under Catholic control. Not to speak of those who are alien to our faith, it is not every Catholic who is fit to have charge of a public library for Catholic readers. Such an onerous position should be assigned to an educated Catholic who would be as remarkable for his loyalty to his religion as for his literary and intellectual attainments.'[11] By this argument public libraries were to come under Catholic control, and not any old Catholic either, only 'educated' Catholics, who were as loyal to religion as to literature, were to be trusted with such a fundamental job.

This was the problem facing President William T. Cosgrave. He had invited the bishops into the debate, hoping to solve the particular Mayo problem and also to come up with a more general long-term solution while they were at it. Now that they had been consulted on their views, President Cosgrave could hardly have been surprised by their stance. Cumann na nGaedheal's self-image was as the socially conservative 'respectable party' and they were upset to find their position as defenders of the faith usurped by the so-called Republican Party. In many ways Fianna Fáil was still seen as a 'slightly constitutional' organisation at this stage in its development, and it would have been regarded as much less close to the Catholic hierarchy. Fianna Fáil was also seen as much more radical, slightly revolutionary and ever-so-slightly untrustworthy. During the Civil War the Catholic hierarchy had threatened excommunication on the republican anti-Treaty side. Residual distrust lingered between them.

President Cosgrave was, as one biographer put it, 'a conservative Catholic, a friend of the clergy and a frequent visitor to Rome.'[12] In 1925 he had been made a papal knight of the Grand Cross, First Class, of the Order of Pope Pius IX. Although he had close ties to the church, as leader of the government he felt he had to stand up for certain secular values so as not to alarm the substantial Protestant minority in the Free State.

Eamon de Valera was at least as religiously conservative as William T. Cosgrave was. He must have seen the Mayo dispute as a great opportunity to re-position his party, to rid itself of some of the disreputable taint of anti-clerical republicanism, even if it would require some fancy political footwork to avoid the accusation of sectarianism.

If Cumann na nGaedheal was bothered by the criticism it received from the priests of Mayo, it was even more sensitive to the onslaughts from the resurgent right-wing Catholic press, in particular the attacks by the *Catholic Bulletin*. President Cosgrave went so far as to raise this in a letter to Cardinal MacRory of Armagh. Cosgrave deplored 'the attitude of certain periodicals, which by their titles, lead the general public to believe that they are authorised exponents of Catholic doctrine. Though we are aware that these papers have no official sanction, we are also aware that many pious Catholics are misled by the titles of these publications whose comments on government policy, and on government departments, often inaccurate and at times so intemperate as to be violently abusive, have done considerable damage, not merely to the political party associated with government, and have resulted in weakening the respect for authority.'[13]

As one historian describes it, the *Catholic Bulletin* was 'a remarkable monthly publication ... in no way under official ecclesiastical supervision. It may indeed have been a standing embarrassment to the higher echelons of the church in Ireland.'[14]

The *Catholic Bulletin* seemed to be very well connected. Its unsigned editorials often hit a nerve with the increasingly sensitive Cumann na nGaedheal leadership. It was generally believed that many of these anonymous tirades were written by Fr Timothy Corcoran, SJ, who was professor of education at UCD. He was undeniably the dominant influence on the views of the *Catholic Bulletin* at this time,[15] and was also the unofficial leader of the Sinn Féin caucus at the university. He was close to de Valera and was a mentor of John Charles McQuaid, who would later become archbishop of Dublin.[16] Like his fellow Jesuit, Fr Stephen Brown, Fr Timothy Corcoran was not an Irish speaker, despite his strong advocacy of the Irish language.[17]

It would perhaps be unwise to accept the views of the more extreme of the religious journals as typical of public opinion at the time. Certainly, some of the bishops took a much more robust view of the wilder realms of the Catholic press than did the beleaguered government. The Minister for Education, Professor John Marcus O'Sullivan, reported back to Cosgrave that in conversation with

Archbishop Harty of Cashel, he had been told that the archbishop 'didn't pay much attention to criticisms of us [the government] by the *Catholic Bulletin*. And that the government "ought to know enough about politics not to mind them."'[18]

It is easy to overestimate the *Catholic Bulletin's* impact at the time. As one historian puts it, the *Bulletin* 'which appears to have acquired an historical curiosity, perhaps because of its extremism and bombastic pedantry, far in excess of its actual significance at the time of publication, may be viewed as representing merely the most hysterical and distorted fringe of the tradition from which it came.'[19]

As evidence of the independence of the bishops, His Grace Archbishop Harty was also reported to have said, 'Stick to the Local Appointments Commissioners', and gave instances of bribery in respect of appointments of doctors in South Tipperary during his father's life as a 'public man'.[20]

As for the specific Miss Dunbar Harrison issue, the hierarchy did not want to get involved, letting it be known that they considered it a local matter for the local bishops to deal with. After a number of meetings with intermediaries, President Cosgrave, accompanied by his Minister for Education, Professor O'Sullivan, finally got to meet with His Grace, the archbishop of Tuam, on 14 April 1932. Archbishop Gilmartin was somewhat defensive. He emphasised that he had not instigated the crisis, rather it was his troops on the ground and he was not going to undermine them. In a signed memorandum written prior to the meeting he made the following points:

1. I may state at the outset that the action of the library committee was taken independently of me.
2. That action has my approval because I consider that there was a Catholic principle involved and that the library committee was justified in acting as they did in defence of that principle.
3. I could not therefore ask those concerned to go back on the position they have taken up.[21]

While he did not say it outright the impression was given that the archbishop was in a more conciliatory frame of mind than many of his priests. However, he stressed that there was no way that the crisis could be resolved while Miss Dunbar Harrison remained in the post. As he put it, 'To acquiesce in her appointment would be a surrender of the principle involved in the protest.'[22] On this point the archbishop was adamant. If the government could not concede this, they would have to look elsewhere for a solution and the church-state conflict would continue.

Chapter 13

'Justified by stirabout and redeemed by porridge'

In the meeting between Archbishop Gilmartin and President Cosgrave, the archbishop argued that Mayo should be treated as a special case due to its history. As the written memorandum of the meeting recorded, Archbishop Gilmartin was of the opinion that owing to Mayo's particular experience with regard to proselytism, the issue of a Protestant librarian in Mayo was seen as an exceptionally sensitive case.

The *Catholic Bulletin* yet again gave vivid expression to Mayo's distinctive past. 'The Catholics of Mayo,' it wrote, 'know well the uses made of the Irish language as an instrument of perversion by organised souperism in their county ever since the Achill mission was started by Souper Nangle and Souper Dallas and since the apostate Carleton's servile and venal pen was hired by Caesar Otway. They were subsidised and patronised by all the leading academic personages of Trinity College Dublin for many a long year.'[1]

At the Mayo County Council meeting on 27 December, John Morahan linked Miss Dunbar Harrison's appointment to souperism. Certainly, proselytism remained a touchy subject in Mayo due mainly to the folk memory of the Famine years. Many of the evangelical organisations had been established pre-Famine but there is little doubt that the failure of the potato crop in the 1840s led to them becoming much more active. There were few more zealous than Rev. Edward Nangle in Achill.

During the Famine, Achill Island had been one of the most deprived districts in Mayo. It was still a living and bitter memory in Mayo. Brigid Redmond, Mayo's first county librarian, related how she had met an old man in Achill in 1928 who spoke to her in Irish and told her 'about Nangle and his settlement of "jumpers" at Dugort, how he had acquired some acres of moorland and built thereon his church, schools and orphanage to pervert the starving people in the Famine years.'[2]

Given Miss Dunbar Harrison's difficulties, it is ironic that there was a pro-Irish language aspect to Rev. Nangle's activities. He had set up a printing press from which he issued a monthly paper known as the *Achill Herald*. He also published copies of the Bible in Irish. As Brigid Redmond put it, 'Nangle must have spent immense energies and monies on the task, and now the work has withered, and his name is held in bitter execration on the island. An alien culture transplanted to this home of ancient sanctities was fore-doomed to blight.'[3]

Private charities provided much-needed relief during the Famine years but some of them availed of the opportunity to try to convert the poorer Catholics. It was felt that zealot missionaries had used the threat of starvation to force some of most destitute Catholics to change their religion in return for food and shelter. Whatever the motivation, it was crudely seen as starving Irish Catholics being pushed into converting to Protestantism in return for bowls of soup. To be called a 'souper' or a 'jumper' was a mortal insult to a family in Mayo. Even today such a label will raise hackles in most parts of the west of Ireland. While Catholic missionaries abroad were often admired for their zeal, grave exception was taken to any form of Protestant missionary work in Ireland, particularly if it was directed at people who were starving. To have 'taken the soup' was considered a dreadful slur on any family's good name. To convert to Protestantism just to survive was to betray one's heritage. The actual number of families who 'converted' remains uncertain, though it would seem that long-term conversions were quite rare. However, whatever the number involved, there is little doubt that such activity created enormous bitterness. The blatant linking of famine relief and proselytising campaigns added insult and degradation to the threat of starvation. Never the quickest county to forgive and forget, this bitterness was to remain long in the memory of the Mayo people.

To coincide with the political crisis over Miss Dunbar Harrison's appointment, the *Catholic Bulletin* ran a historical feature on 'A Souper Library in Mayo'. The article was actually about a 'souper school' in Ballindine rather than a library, but it served the *Bulletin's* purpose, reminding those who may have forgotten, of notorious proselytisers like Rev. Nangle.

Rev. Edward Nangle's Achill mission had actually been established in 1831. The Famine had merely added impetus to his missionary efforts. The local priest claimed that his parishioners 'were dying of hunger and rather than die they have submitted to his [Nangle's] impious tenets.'

Rev. Alexander Dallas and his Irish Church Missions were active in Connemara, one of the poorest areas in Ireland during the height of the Famine period. As Desmond Bowen put it, 'there is no doubt about the terrible purity of Dallas's motives. He was out to save souls – not to give temporal relief to the suffering Irish people.'

An account by Mrs Dallas of an incident in Errismore gives some insight into his detachment from the suffering happening all around him.

> We walked across to Mannin Bay and on our way we saw about a dozen poor famished creatures attempting to work, but too weak to do anything. It was impossible to lose the opportunity of telling the Gospel to these apparently dying men as they stood or sat around me like living skeletons. They listened with fixed attention, as if they were pausing on the brink of the grave to receive a message from heaven as to their journey beyond it. I never set forth the salvation of Christ under so strong a feeling that my hearers would be soon called to experience the truth of my statement.

With such attitudes it is unsurprising that the activities of Rev.

Dallas and his Irish Church Missions were the cause of much bitterness in Connacht.

Harriet Martineau, a not entirely unbiased English traveller, visited Achill in September 1852. She remarked on the tension on the island. 'For a long course of years there was a quietness which might almost be called peace in Achill.'

She put the blame for the unrest squarely on the shoulders of Archbishop John McHale and the combative clergymen he had sent to the island. She gave a vivid account of a particular incident which had occurred.

> The admitted facts are, according to the report of petty sessions, that the two priests collected the people in the village of Keel (Catholic, and the largest place on the island); that they supported each other in instigating the attack by which a Scripture Reader was stoned, knocked down among the turf, and beaten; that one of the priests, foaming at the mouth with passion, called the readers 'damned devils' , and the Protestants 'jumper devils' and 'stirabout jumpers'; that he charged the parents with sending their children to school to lose their souls, to be 'justified by stirabout and redeemed by porridge'; that he bade the people 'scald, scald' and 'persecute to death' the Protestants of Achill; that he pronounced the curse of God on any one who should sell them a pint of milk or a stone of potatoes; that he said he had but one life, and he, 'would willingly give it to drive out these devils, and see Achill great, glorious and free, as it was before they came.

It was little wonder that Nangle moved from Achill soon after this incident.

Bishop Thomas Plunket became Protestant Bishop of the united dioceses of Tuam, Killala and Achonry in 1839. He was also landlord of an estate in Tourmakeady. He used his power to support both Nangle and Dallas, and in fact gave Nangle a position at the rectory of Skreen in North Mayo.

In the post-Famine years he was heavily influential in the promotion of missionary and evangelical Protestantism in Connacht.

The Bishop and his sister, Catherine Plunket, set up a Protestant school in Tourmakeady. He came into conflict with the Catholic priest in the area, Fr Peter Ward, and then with Ward's successor, Fr Patrick Lavelle.

'The point of a crowbar'

The struggle between them became popularly known as 'the war in Partry'. It flared up in 1860. Plunket was accused of using his power as a landlord to proselytise, that 'he preached his gospel at the point of a crowbar', that is, that if his tenants refused to allow their children attend Catherine Plunket's school, they would be evicted.

Plunket's Tourmakeady estate agent defended him, admitting that, while there had been evictions they were not due to religion. The people evicted were guilty of 'outrage, conspiracy, incendiarism and murder.' The incident had come to the attention of the *London Times*. It was critical of Plunket's estate policy. As they put it, 'Lord Plunket applies to all alike a punishment which is too severe for the innocent, as it is insufficient for the guilty.'

In the 1920s, some Protestant ministers made the tentative suggestion that use of the word 'souper' was, at the very least, indelicate if not downright distasteful and that it should perhaps be withdrawn from the vocabulary of the Catholic press. Conservative periodicals such as the *Catholic Bulletin* and the *Catholic Mind* would have none of it.

In 1906 the contentious issue of Bibles in Irish had been the cause of a minor controversy in Dublin corporation libraries, when two members of the municipal council (one of them the MP T.M. Harrington) had 'denounced the Hibernian Bible Society for having given, and the Libraries Committee for having accepted', a Bible in Irish for each library branch. The Hibernian Bible Society was accused of being a proselytising institution. 'The discussion in the corporation was seized upon by the Dublin press as an event beyond ordinary importance for sale of copy.' The Books Committee found it necessary to defend itself. It claimed that it had 'always acted upon the principle that public libraries should be public libraries in fact as well as in name, and consequently that they should not be administered as if by the ignorant in any narrow, bigoted or intolerant spirit: that the libraries are the property of all the citizens.'[4]

In October 1906, the full meeting of the corporation backed this policy. 'The report of the Libraries Committee was adopted without a division and by an overwhelming majority. The opponents … could be counted upon the fingers of one hand.' The controversy quickly fizzled out.

As well as souperism and Bibles in Irish, Seán na Sagart had also been mentioned in the County Council debates. Seán na Sagart's infamy went even further back in time. He had a fearsome reputation as a demon from Mayo's folk memory, a bogeyman rendered all the more scary in that he was based on a real person. Seán na Sagart (John of the Priests) had been a legendary priest hunter during penal times. So infamous was he that in America his nickname, Seán na Sagart, was used as a generic name for all priest hunters. Many tales were attached to this legend.

In a Catholic Truth Society booklet from 1946, R.J. Bennett laid out the accepted facts of Seán na Sagart's life. His real name was John Mullowney. He was a native of Ballintubber Parish, from the townland of Skehanagh, near Ballyheane. As a youth in Mayo he had led a life of dissolution. He had expensive taste that could not be supported by legal means. He was reputed to have two particular vices, drinking and stealing horses. He was only of average height but he carried himself in a fashion that made him seem taller than he really was, while his whole bearing was indicative of strength. Brown-eyed, under shaggy eyebrows, he could be good company. He was free with his ill-gotten gains, always anxious to pour strong liquor down his throat.

John Mullowney was little more than a boy when he was captured and sentenced to death in Castlebar for horse stealing. He was so contemptuous of his fatal sentence that he attracted the attention of the prison authorities. They offered him a free pardon provided he join the ranks of the priest hunters. It was an occupation for which he proved to have an exceptional aptitude.[5] It was reported that on one occasion he lured a priest to him by pretending to his sister that he was mortally ill. His sister, Nancy Louhnan, was a devout Catholic. She had been widowed at the age of twenty-five and had two infant daughters. Her brother asked her to find a priest for him so he could repent his sins and confess. When the priest turned up, he promptly turned him in for the bounty. One particular priest he was hunting, Andrew Higgins, was reputed to have been killed by a pistol shot as he was being pushed off in a currach near Pulnathacken.

John Mullowney eventually met his end while in epic pursuit of Fr David Bourke. He chased the friar from Ballintubber on through Kiltharshahawn, Derreenfaderring, Skeeh and Furnace, on to the high road towards Cloonach and Ballynew, finishing up at Aill Baile Nuaid near Partry.[6] It was there that the tables were turned and the hunter became the hunted. In the ensuing struggle John Mullowney was killed. He was stabbed to death, some say by a relative of Andrew Higgins, the priest he had killed. The place of his death is marked by a tall stone in a wood near Partry. According to Matthew Archdeacon, whose novel based on John Mullowney's story was published in 1844, 'The deeply blood-stained priest hunter who seemed through life to have neither loved nor feared God or man' was interred in a little dismantled chapel adjacent to Ballintubber Abbey.[7] Even then he achieved no peace. Outraged locals were said to have dug up his grave and scattered his bones, throwing them into the waters of Lough Carra. The ash tree that shadowed John Mullowney's grave was long an article of curiosity to Ballintubber visitors. It was a deformed branchless and leafless trunk, 'an object of awe as well as of wonder among the peasantry of the district.'[8] Whatever the precise truth of all these stories there is no doubt they were widely circulated in Mayo.

It might seem excessive to lay the guilt for all this history at the feet of Miss Dunbar Harrison, but Archbishop Gilmartin felt that Mayo's past had such a strong influence on its current political reality that the wrath of his priests and their flock was justified.

While the government made little progress in their endeavours to solve the specific dispute in Mayo, there were also discussions on the general issue of libraries and how they should be run. A proposal was floated that responsibility for the library system in the Free State be taken out of the hands of the local authorities and run instead by central government. However, the bishops made a counter-suggestion that the library service should be treated in a similar fashion to the school system. In the Free State at the time, schools came under clerical control. Libraries would be subject to a form of denominational apartheid. Protestant libraries for Protestant people, and separate Catholic libraries for Catholic people. If libraries were seen as solely educational institutions, this was perhaps the logical extension of that line of reasoning but it was not one that President Cosgrave could agree to. He threatened to resign if the bishops forced him to make a decision on this issue, as did another member of his cabinet, Desmond Fitzgerald, who had also been involved in the negotiations.

It would be a mistake, however, to believe that the government was without support in its stance. An editorial in the *Enniscorthy Echo* declared, 'As a Catholic country we give control of education, so far as Catholics are concerned, to the Catholic church, and from that some people argued that the library service, being an educational service, should be strictly Catholic. But a library service is primarily a social amenity and can no more be called an educational service than a theatre or a picture house.

'It may and does serve an educational purpose, but unless it is a specialised or propaganda library its educational aspect is only incidental. The average user of a general library reads to amuse himself, not primarily for educational purposes.'[9]

The Church of Ireland Gazette took a much less combative stance on the dispute than had *The Irish Times*. In December 1930 the *Gazette* welcomed 'various indications that Fianna Fáil is growing more moderate and less prone to adventures. We welcome also the declaration, by some of its spokesmen (in connection with the Mayo librarian case), that they intend to give fair play to all Irish people irrespective of their religious beliefs.'[10] One week later the *Gazette* returned to the issue. 'The Free State Minister for Local Government,' it wrote, 'has given Mayo County Council an opportunity to reconsider its attitude at a meeting to be held by the end of this year but makes it plain that the government will insist on the appointment of Miss Dunbar as librarian for the county.'[11] The *Gazette* seemed content to trust the Cumann na nGaedheal government to protect the rights of the Protestant minority in the Free State. Wary of their place in the newly formed country, they tended to keep a low profile when it came to controversies such as this.

In her book *The Church of Ireland Community of Killala and Achonry, 1870-1940*, Miriam Moffitt writes that 'with the establishment of the Free State, the Protestant community felt more isolated from the affairs of state than ever before. The victimisation of Protestants in the early days of the Irish Free State persuaded many to move to Northern Ireland, or to emigrate. Those who remained became, of necessity, a silent minority.'[12] Little wonder that it was so, given Miss Dunbar Harrison's experience in Mayo.

Chapter 14

'The worst thing since Cromwell'

The Irish language, ostensibly the reason for the furore surrounding Letitia Dunbar Harrison's appointment, tended to get lost in the ensuing debate. Most of the letters published concentrated on Miss Dunbar Harrison's religion or her Trinity College education. As previously mentioned, Kathleen White had a similar lack of Irish yet this did not prove a barrier to her being appointed as librarian in Leitrim. However, it would be a mistake to think that the language aspect was overlooked entirely. Rev. Malachy Mac Branain, PP, Ahascragh, was one of those who focused on it.

> As one who many years ago took a successful part in the fight for compulsory Irish in the National University, allow me to express my wholehearted appreciation of the action of the Co. Mayo library committee in refusing to accept the recommendation of the Local Appointments Commissioners to the effect that a graduate of Trinity College should be appointed as librarian for the Irish-speaking Co. Mayo.
>
> … The Local Appointments Commissioners by their action in this and similar cases are giving a new lease of influence and power to Trinity College and to the West British ideals it was founded to establish.
>
> The procedure is inconsistent with the principle of compulsory Irish advocated by the government of An Saorstát and most unfair to the National University and its constituent colleges … To make the position still more inconsistent the chairman of the Gaeltacht Commission, Gen. Mulcahy, is the member of the government responsible for insisting that the person appointed as librarian for the Irish-speaking Co. Mayo must be a graduate of Trinity College.
>
> It is difficult to understand how our people have tolerated this whole policy of centralisation, which in practice has taken away from our local representatives on public boards whatever powers they had, and transferred those powers to an unknown body in Dublin, who are responsible to nobody.

The policy is opposed to all democratic principles and is the exact opposite of what we would expect from a new government, which after years of foreign domination now claims to have full control of its own affairs ... The rights of the people ... have been handed over to an intolerant minority, whose real sentiments regarding this country have been so eloquently expressed by the Protestant archbishops of Armagh and Dublin, in their recent pronouncement on the veto of the English Privy Council over all the disputed questions in the Free State.[1]

The *Catholic Bulletin* had always taken a hard-line stance when it came to the question of Irish identity. This excerpt from an editorial in 1924 gives a flavour of its attitude. 'The Irish nation,' the *Catholic Bulletin* wrote, 'is the Gaelic nation, its language and literature is the Gaelic language; its history is the history of the Gael.'[2] The question of the Irish language and Miss Dunbar Harrison was by no means black and white. Even the Irish language organisations were split on the issue. As the *Cork Examiner* reported, the Gaelic League received a letter from Rev. Mac Evilly, Claremorris, in which he stated that in his opinion 'the appointment of a commissioner for Mayo was the best thing for the Irish language that has happened yet. He had had a conversation with the commissioner, P.J. Bartley, who asked him to suggest two members of the Gaelic League and two members of the Gaelic Athletic Association for membership of the Vocational Education Committee.'

'I complained that the old vocational committee had dropped the scheme of scholarships in the Gaeltacht,' he said.

Commissioner Bartley had promised to remedy this situation. Rev. Mac Evilly concluded that 'he is the first friend the Irish language has had on the county committee.'[3]

The chairman of the meeting, Seán Ó hÚadaigh, said that the reason why the Gaelic League had not intervened in the public debate about the Mayo librarianship was because they knew that the people who were taking part were not friends of the Irish language.

The dispute did not go away and later that year the annual

congress of the Gaelic League passed a motion 'that a change should be made in the methods of the Public Appointments Commissioners because by their selection of applicants for public posts, they were not doing justice to Irish'. Mr Ó Maoláin, who proposed the motion, referred specifically to the Mayo case. Mr P. O'Mulkerrin, Killaloe, said that the appointment of the librarian for County Mayo was one of the worst things done since Cromwell. *The Irish Times* were so taken by the phrase that they used it as the headline for their report on the congress.[4]

The Gaelic League was formed in 1893 to promote knowledge and interest in the Irish language. That the Mayo librarian controversy had posed problems for it is evident from another motion discussed at their 1931 congress. A motion from the Pádraig Pearse branch was moved requesting the congress to condemn the action of those who prevented discussion at the executive committee of the appointment of a non-Irish speaking librarian for a post in the Gaeltacht, as the objectives of the league were not advanced on that occasion.[5] Mr O'Mulkerrin, seconding the motion, said that when the executive committee was negligent in matters affecting the language and nationality, other organisations could not be blamed. Seán Ó hÚadaigh, who had presided over the December 1930 meeting of the executive committee referred to in the motion of censure, said he had accepted a number of motions on the issue but had declined to accept another resolution because a portion of it was connected not with the Gaelic League but with political and state matters. He believed then, as he still did, that his decision was correct. There were in the Gaelic League persons of different religions. When the question of the Mayo appointment was first raised, it was based on the principle of the language, but after that the religious aspect had been raised and it had assumed a larger degree of attention than the language itself. He made no apology for his action. Mr McGinley said that he thought the congress ought to thank the executive committee for its action in the matter, and for declining to drag religion into the discussion. The motion was defeated by a large majority.[6]

The ructions in the Gaelic League reflect certain unease among some language enthusiasts who felt that language was being used as a pawn in a political game. As Councillor Pat O'Hara pointed out, a stricter regulation was being used in Miss Dunbar Harrison's case. The language requirement was a law more honoured in the breach than the observance and there were numerous cases of staff in local authorities who had been allowed take up their posts while being unable to speak Irish. Many were also uncomfortable with the support Irish was getting from people who had previously shown no great interest in reviving the language. Dean D'Alton's attitude to Irish at the library committee meeting had been somewhat resentful of its compulsory requirement for certain jobs. He had made the flippant joke with regard to blacksmiths being required to know Irish, it was a wonder the horses weren't expected to know the language as well. As one eminent Irish historian has pointed out, Dean D'Alton was not an entirely uncritical supporter of literature in Irish. At one time he even persuaded the Mayo library committee to ban the books of Pádraig Pearse.[7]

This was a common thread in arguments amongst proponents of the Irish language. *An Phoblacht*, the Sinn Féin newspaper, had been supportive of the original rejection of Miss Dunbar Harrison. 'Every Irish nationalist,' the newspaper wrote, 'was behind the Mayo County Council when it refused to accept the Staters' Jobs Commission's appointment of a non-Gaelic speaker to a Gaeltacht position.'[8] *An Phoblacht*, however, deplored what they saw as the cynical opportunism of many of her critics. It condemned the introduction of the sectarian argument 'by such anti-Irish exponents as the Very Rev. Canon D'Alton. He and his friends have been soundly trounced now by the very party which they helped to place in power. As for Canon D'Alton and his confrères – Devil mend them.'[9]

One of the most eloquent speeches given at the Mayo County Council meeting was by J.T. Morahan. However, 'the indignation expressed about the appointment of a non-Irish speaker as librarian for Mayo would prove no bar to Mr Morahan successfully proposing a candidate for a post as teacher, despite her lack of Irish [in 1932].'[10]

Many people had an ambivalent attitude towards the Irish language; they wished to speak their native tongue yet were unable to do so. It was an aspiration rather than a reality. In general more people claimed to speak Irish and understand it than actually did. It was more alive in theory than in practice.

At the special meeting of Mayo County Council on 27 December 1930 just two speakers used Irish, Councillors Munnelly and Campbell, even though the language issue was the apparent cause of the crisis. The meeting received extensive coverage in the local papers; yet, none of them carried the text of the speeches in Irish. For instance *The Connaught Telegraph* merely stated that 'Mr John Munnelly spoke in very eloquent Irish', leading one to believe that the newspapers knew their readership would not be able to read big blocks of text in Irish or else it was simply that their reporters did not understand the language well enough to transcribe it.[11]

Fr Stephen J. Brown, SJ, sponsor of Ellen Burke and librarian of the Central Catholic Library, was the author of a number of books on Irish literature. In the introduction to his *Guide to Books on Ireland* he explained that one of the reasons why he hadn't included books in the Irish language on his list was that his 'own knowledge of the Irish language is not yet sufficient to enable me even to edit notes of books in Irish.'[12] In Brown's preface to *Ireland in Fiction*, the first edition of which was 'destroyed by fire in the course of the Rising in Dublin at Easter 1916', Brown repeated this explanation, adding the comment, 'Nevertheless, the omission of books in the Irish language from a guide to Irish fiction remains an anomaly, one of the many anomalies produced by the historic causes that have all but destroyed the Irish language as the living speech of Ireland.'[13]

Canon Hegarty from Belmullet, who spoke against Miss Dunbar Harrison's appointment at the meetings of the Mayo library committee, was no great devotee of the Irish language either. He was reported to have referred to Irish language classes in the Gaeltacht as cesspools of infamy.

To a certain extent the problem was of the government's own making. In 1928 it had issued an order that all future appointees to local government positions in Gaeltacht areas would be required to demonstrate sufficient knowledge of Irish to enable them to conduct their business through the medium of the language. Initially only tradesmen and labourers were to be exempt but the list of exemptions was extended at a later date as the basic unreality of the measure dawned on the government.[14] There were simply not enough qualified speakers of the language to fill the various positions, in particular, specialised ones like that of county librarian. In one of the many ironies that political life throws up, it was Richard Mulcahy, the minister in charge of a commission for the promotion of the Irish language, who originally came up with the proposal and who then, as Minister for Local Government, must have felt honour-bound to implement it. Yet Mayo was a Gaeltacht area, so designated. It did have a substantial Irish-speaking population around Tourmakeady and also some pockets of Irish speakers around Erris in the north of Mayo.

The Irish language had been exploited by evangelical Protestants in the past and a deep sense of distrust now pervaded. As the ever-zealous *Catholic Bulletin* put it, 'Mayo knows well and remembers well the uses made of the Irish language by many emissaries of Trinity College Dublin, from Ballina to Ballaghderreen, from Dugort to Tourmakeady in the epoch 1820 to 1870.'[15]

For many, language was a badge of identity and the reason that Miss Dunbar Harrison was turned down was not so much that she didn't speak Irish but because of what that represented. She was an outsider. Language was simply just an obvious manifestation of this difference. As F.S. Lyons argued, it was a case of 'Irish Ireland versus Anglo-Irish Ireland ... Catholicism and Gaelicism, and the nationalism they nourished, were reacting primarily against England. It was English manners and morals, English influences, English Protestantism, English rule, that they sought to eradicate.'[16]

John O'Mahony of the Fenian movement had stated many years previously that 'our duty is to de-Anglicise Ireland, Gaelicise Ireland and Catholicise Ireland.' It was Letitia Dunbar Harrison's bad fortune that she had become entangled in one of the skirmishes of that unfinished conflict.

Chapter 15

'I take the Ten Commandments as my code'

Up to this time the procedures of the Local Appointments Commission had been treated as confidential. However, following the legal advice of the attorney general, John A. Costello, the government compelled the Commission to pass on detailed reports of the selection procedure in the Mayo librarian case, some of which President Cosgrave revealed in his Dáil statement of 11 December 1931. During the 1928 Dáil debate on the workings of the LAC, President Cosgrave and Minister Ernest Blythe had placed great emphasis on the necessity of a guarantee of strict confidentiality in order for the LAC to do its work properly. However, due to the pressure of circumstances, the government now reversed its stance.

In his statement Cosgrave took the Dáil through the various steps the LAC had taken with regard to easing the requirement for the Irish language. He also made it known that the selection board was made up of Catholics and that the other four successful candidates at the time were also Catholics. Further details of the workings of the LAC and its interview procedure were disclosed to the Catholic hierarchy at a later date. It was also divulged that, despite protestations to the contrary in her letter, Miss Ellen Burke had failed the Irish language test. In fact, the state papers reveal that the government gathered much more detailed information from the Local Appointments Commission, including not only the procedures used and the make-up of the selection board but also the exact marks received by the candidates at interview.[1]

It is worthwhile to examine the recruitment procedure in more depth. On 12 February 1930, the advertisement was first issued to the press. As was customary at the time all the existing county librarian vacancies were listed together. They would be the subject of one set of interviews rather than a separate round of interviews for each vacancy. There were four vacant posts in Carlow, Kilkenny, Mayo and Cavan. On 4 May 1930 the initial interviews were held. James Montgomery, the film censor, chaired the board. The other members were W.J. Williams, lecturer, UCD, Christina Keogh, librarian, Irish Central Library for Students, Richard Hayes, senior assistant librarian, National Library and Thomas E. Gay, librarian, Capel Street Library. Nineteen candidates were called for interview and at the end of the proceedings just four were deemed to be 'technically qualified and competent.'[2] The successful candidates were all female. Taken in descending order, Iona M. McLeod, Brigid Barron, Letitia Dunbar Harrison and Kathleen M. White all passed the interview.

However, the latter two were deemed not to have competent Irish. The first two had sufficient Irish and were offered their choice of which county librarian post they wished to take. This might seem unusual but this was the practice at the time. As an *Irish Independent* report put it, 'The board placed the candidates in the order of merit, and the Local Appointments Commission then, according to the custom which obtains in connection with the filling of all vacancies where more than one exists, invited the candidates first on the list to take a choice, and so on, until there was only one post to be filled.'[3] Iona McLeod elected to go to Carlow and Brigid Barron to Kilkenny. As Miss Dunbar Harrison and Miss White had failed the Irish element of the selection process the Mayo and Cavan posts were left unfilled.

On 15 May 1930 the vacant posts for the two counties were re-advertised along with two more vacancies in the newly established library services of Meath and Leitrim. These counties had recently adopted the Public Libraries Act and were looking for their first librarian. Presumably, the reason for this flurry of activity was that the Carnegie Trust had set the end of 1930 as the deadline to avail of their grant scheme for rural library schemes. It was decided that those who had applied for the original vacancies did not have to re-apply and also that the same interview board would be used. The interviews were organised for 12 July 1930. However, at short notice Mr Montgomery was not available due to business commitments so the interviews went ahead without him, with Mr Williams as chair of the four-person interview board. It was also decided neither to re-interview any of the candidates from the first round of interviews nor to charge them the application fee, not unless their circumstances had changed in the meantime. In the case of one candidate, Feargus MacMurchadha, who had attained a library qualification since the first round of interviews, it was decided that he would be re-interviewed.

In all, nine candidates were called to interview on the second occasion, on 12 July 1930. By this time Waterford had adopted the Public Libraries Act so there was a post available there also. The selection board produced five successful candidates and listed them in the following order (the marks are out of a possible total of 700).

> Mary McNevin – 530
> Gerald Guise-Brown – 365
> Feargus MacMurchadha – 360
> Letitia Dunbar Harrison – 320
> Kathleen White – 280[4]

As on the previous occasion, the successful candidates were given their choice of the vacancies in order of merit. Mary McNevin opted for Meath, Gerald Guise-Brown for Cavan and Feargus MacMurchadha went for Waterford. After the first three had exercised their choice Letitia Dunbar Harrison chose Mayo and by process of elimination Kathleen White was left with Leitrim.[5] To modern eyes it might seem a somewhat unusual way of filling vacancies but it was the method commonly used by the Local Appointments Commission at the time whenever there were a number of vacancies available. The leader of the Labour Party, Mayo TD T.J. O'Connell, was particularly critical of this procedure. It was also pointed out that if the successful candidates who were deemed to have good Irish were allocated to Gaeltacht counties the original controversy would have been averted.

While Irish was a requirement for many civil service and local authority jobs, in reality there was a shortage of people with sufficient knowledge of the language. Libraries were no exception. An *Irish Independent* journalist was told by a well-placed government source that 'persons with a real training in library work and who know Irish are very few.'[6] It was for this reason that the LAC relaxed the requirement between the first and second set of interviews, an action that later fuelled many conspiracy theories.

President Cosgrave indicated in his Dáil statement of 11 December 1930 that the selection board had been made up of people of the Catholic faith. It could in fact be said of James Montgomery, the chairman of the board that interviewed Letitia Dunbar Harrison, that he was a devout and conservative Catholic. Formerly an employee of the Dublin Gas Company, James Montgomery served as official film censor from 1923 to 1940.[7] He was in many ways a deeply committed Christian. Describing his attitude to his role as censor he was not reticent about his religious motivation.

'I take the Ten Commandments as my code,' he declared.[8]

'The Los Anglicisation of Ireland'

James Montgomery had also gone on the record to assert that he feared, not the Anglicisation of Ireland, but rather the Los Anglicisation of Ireland. In his first year as censor it was said that he had watched over ten thousand miles of film. This may have been an exaggeration, though there was no doubt that he was an avid fan of the cinema. His friends 'chaffed him' that he still spent a great deal of his spare time going to 'the pictures' as an ordinary spectator.[9]

The general opinion of Mr Montgomery was that he was a conservative Catholic and that his role as censor frustrated him in that he did not have the legal powers to impose a more rigid film-censorship policy. The ultra-traditionalist *Catholic Mind* had even awarded Mr Montgomery its seal of approval for his work. The journal said of him that 'he has, within his powers, done everything possible to clean the cinemas. He is one of the most courageous Catholic actionists in Ireland.'[10]

A graduate of Queen's College Galway, W.J. Williams obtained both a higher diploma and a masters in education from UCD. From 1914 to 1924 he was a tutor and supervisor at All Hallows College and was also on the lecturing staff of the College of Science. Following the amalgamation of the College of Science with UCD he became a lecturer in education. During the 1930s Mr Williams was the clerk of convocation with the National University of Ireland. In 1943 he was appointed as chair of education in UCD. In a curious coincidence a controversy arose over his knowledge of the Irish language. The Gaelic League protested at his lack of fluency. 'The College made clear, however, despite the Gaelic League's vigorous objection, that even in so crucial an appointment as the most influential chair of education in the country, academic criteria counted for more than strictly national requirements. After a brief but very ill-tempered controversy Professor Williams was confirmed in his appointment.'[11]

Professor Williams' role as chair of education was approved by the senate of NUI by twenty-three votes to seven. This was in spite of the National University Convocation urging his rejection by one hundred and one votes to ninety-four.[12] The other members of the selection board all had distinguished careers in the area of librarianship.

'The war of brains'
In 1930 Richard Hayes was an assistant librarian with the National

Library. By the end of the decade he had become its director. During the Second World War he was recruited by the Irish army's head of intelligence, Colonel Bryan, to act as an interrogator and code breaker. Hayes was a War of Independence veteran who was both a self-taught codes and ciphers expert and a distinguished linguist.

According to one historian of the period, his code-breaking 'achievements during the Emergency have frequently been distorted, yet the documentary evidence indicates that in real terms they have not been exaggerated.'[13] In fact the British came to realize that Richard Hayes was so exceptionally able as a cryptographer that he had, in fact broken their code messages from London. Of Hayes' code-breaking skills it was said by Cecil Liddell, the British head of MI5's Irish section that 'his gifts in this direction amounted almost to genius.' As Hayes himself asserted, in the 'unseen war of brains between the cipher makers and cipher breakers … the cipher breakers won.'[14]

Hayes worked in the National Library in the mornings, then got on his bicycle and rode up to Collins Barracks where he collected the night's harvest of messages and decoded them. He was assisted by three army lieutenants who had no special knowledge of cryptography. Hayes was also involved in the interrogation of any German spies captured during the course of the Emergency.

Despite Ireland's so-called neutrality, there was a great deal of co-operation with their British counterparts. As Liddell put it 'there was no doubt that this co-ordination was largely due to Colonel Bryan's enthusiasm as an intelligence officer and to Dr Hayes' cryptographic zeal. It is very doubtful if his military superiors agreed to the passing of the ciphers to the British and certainly his political superiors would not have done so.'

'An inconspicuous librarian'
Tom Gay, the Capel Street librarian, had been a member of the Irish Republican Army and was reportedly a key figure in Michael

Collins' extensive intelligence network during the War of Independence. Four Dublin Castle officials had been recruited by Michael Collins: Ned Broy, James MacNamara, Joe Kavanagh and David Neligan. 'During their weekly debriefings, these agents passed valuable information at a Dublin safehouse owned by Tom Gay, an inconspicuous librarian.'[15] As David Neligan himself put it in his autobiography, 'Broy, McNamara and myself used to meet Collins once a week in the house of Tommy Gay, 8 Haddon Road, Clontarf … The three of us G-men travelled separately on trams to Gay's house. Collins generally cycled on an ancient machine.'[16] Not only was Tom Gay's house used as a meeting point but so was his place of employment, Capel Street Library, which was conveniently close, just across the river from Dublin Castle.[17]

'A bookworm openly'

David Neligan described Tom Gay as 'a tiny Dublin man, with bronchial trouble which made his life a burden … he led a double life, a bookworm openly and also, secretly, a confidential courier for Collins. He was so unobtrusive that neither the library nor his home came under suspicion. I often left urgent messages in the library and one could be sure of their prompt and safe delivery. As I pushed my way through a lot of down-and-outs who frequented the reading-room it used to strike me that the place would be the last to be suspected by the British and I was right.'[18]

This inconspicuous librarian was also a committed trade unionist. He was a member of the Irish Local Government Officers' Trade Union (which later became the Irish Local Government Officials' Union). Tom Gay served on the union's national executive, as well as acting as chairman of its Dublin corporation branch. So prominent was he in the ILGOTU that he was elected as its honorary president on 12 June 1927 at City Hall, Cork.[19]

Tom Gay was considered 'a polished and fluent speaker … [who] was frequently sought to support often forlorn causes and rarely failed to turn up and give his earnest and sincere support. He possessed an extraordinary energy and unselfishly devoted prolonged periods to intensive efforts.'[20]

Mr Gay left the library service during the Emergency to act as Director of Air Raid Precautions (ARP) for Dublin. He subsequently worked as private secretary for the Dublin city manager. Mr Gay seems to have been a bundle of energy. He was also involved with the Gaelic League and the Gaelic Athletic Association and was one of the founders of the Camogie League. He must have been a busy man at the turn of the decade because he was also heavily concerned with the newly formed professional body representing librarianship in Ireland, the Library Association of Ireland. He became chairman of the executive board of the LAI and was joint-editor of *An Leabharlann*, the organisation's magazine.

'The starling and the stork'

Christina Keogh, who had also served on the selection board, was an influential member of the LAI. She acted as its honorary treasurer for twenty-two years and went on to become its first woman president in 1958. The Irish Central Library for Students was founded in 1923 and Miss Keogh was appointed librarian. 'She was a small slender woman,' Dermot Foley wrote of her in an article in *An Leabharlann*, 'whose frail physique was incapable, one would have said, of absorbing the punishment inseparable from the offices she held. But Chrissy Keogh was made of tough material with a gift for amusement.'[21]

Miss Keogh also worked with the Carnegie Trust in Ireland as librarian and technical adviser in association with the Trust's organising librarian, that languid man of the theatre, Lennox Robinson. 'To see them walk together along Merrion Square,' commented Dermot Foley, 'was something to remember, and I have cause to remember it, for, impertinent brat that I was, I addressed them as the starling and the stork. Instead of being mortally offended, this chirpy slip of a girl looked skywards at the melancholy height beside her and laughed outright.'[22]

After Lennox Robinson's enforced resignation in 1924, Miss Keogh continued her work with the Carnegie Trust without him. 'We who have grown up with the county schemes,' wrote Dermot Foley, 'of which she was attendant nurse from the cradle of poverty in which they were born, must ever feel grateful that a dedicated officer was at the heart of the whole affair managed by her and Robinson for the Carnegie Trust.'[23]

The situation was made difficult for the LAI in that Fr Stephen J. Brown, SJ, was also a member of the executive board. A writer of numerous guides to literature, Fr Brown was nevertheless an unabashed supporter of censorship. His Catholicism was paramount. 'As for the rights of art and literature,' he once said, 'Neither has any rights against God.'[24] His rationale was that 'as we know in English-speaking countries, Ireland not excluded, Catholics have to live in a mental climate that is far from being Catholic. We must be inoculated against it; we must take measures so that the climatic conditions may not offset our spiritual health.'[25]

Fr Brown was a lecturer in the School of Library Training, University College Dublin. He held strong views on the role of the librarian. In his book, *Libraries and Literature from a Catholic Standpoint*, he writes, 'It is when one comes to realise the power and influence wielded, however unobtrusively and indirectly, by the librarian, that one becomes convinced of the importance to religion in its wider sense of the conscience that is behind that power and influence. Catholics claim no monopoly of conscientiousness, nor even of the Christian conscience, but they certainly have clearer principles to guide their conscience and usually a better training in these principles. I submit that Christianity and public morality have much to gain by the presence of Catholic librarians in public libraries across the world.'[26]

Fr Brown was librarian of the Central Catholic Library where Miss Ellen Burke had been employed, and it was he who had suggested she write a letter to Dean D'Alton, the infamous letter that was read out at the special meeting of Mayo County Council and that was subsequently published nationally.

One might conjecture that Tom Gay and Christina Keogh felt precluded from drawing attention to the Mayo controversy at the executive-board level of the Library Association as they were interested parties, having sat on the selection board for the Appointments Commission. However, given the level of debate at national level, with libraries literally front-page news, the LAI could hardly avoid the issue either. In reality it was not quite so straightforward.

The first stirring of debate at board level was at the Library Association's meeting on 17 December 1930. A motion critical of the Local Appointments Commission and its recruitment procedures was tabled. It was quickly sidelined in favour of a compromise proposal. It was agreed to send a delegation from the LAI to meet with the LAC to discuss their concerns. The carefully chosen three-person deputation included both Tom Gay and Fr Brown.[27] At the next executive meeting, on 16 January 1931, Tom Gay, in his capacity as joint-editor of *An Leabharlann*, submitted for the consideration of the board an article dealing with the Mayo dispute, which he suggested should appear as an editorial. However, John Roy proposed and was seconded by Fr Brown, 'that without prejudice to the statements made in Mr Gay's article, no reference whatever be made to the Mayo controversy in the next issue of *An Leabharlann*.' The minutes of the meeting give no reason for their opposition nor were any details given of the ensuing debate but on a show of hands the resolution was passed by six votes for to three against.[28]

Mr Gay's editorial was blocked. He promptly tendered his resignation as joint-editor of the magazine. It was a delicately gauged reaction by Tom Gay. He stepped down as editor but he chose to remain on in the more important role of chairman of the executive board.

The Library Association had been formed in 1928. Among its aims were to promote libraries in Ireland and 'to promote whatever may tend to the improvement of the position or qualifications of librarians.'[29] This makes it all the more remarkable that it took no public stance on the Mayo librarian case. Despite their silence on the Mayo issue the LAI saw fit to comment on what had happened in Leitrim. Again, at the instigation of Tom Gay, a motion expressing disquiet at what had transpired was passed at a meeting of the executive council on 23 January 1931. It viewed 'with great concern the action of Leitrim County Council in rescinding at its meeting on 3 January, its earlier resolution to adopt the Public Libraries Act, and it earnestly hopes that the Leitrim County Council will, in order to promote the general welfare and cultural interests of the people of the county, reconsider its decision.'[30] Tom Gay proposed this resolution and, according to the official minutes of the LAI, it was unanimously adopted. However, this was not the whole story. The *Irish Independent* gave a different slant to what had transpired. The paper reported that the original motion proposed had been amended at the meeting. Fr Stephen J. Brown, SJ, it was stated, had argued that the original motion was too specific and that they should make the resolution general, and it should be disassociated altogether from the Mayo business in case it would cause that dispute to spread.[31] There were also fears that if Leitrim treated the resolution with disdain, as they were quite likely to, they might start a chain reaction that would spread to other councils.[32] Presumably the fear was that other counties might decide to rescind their adoption of the Public Libraries Act and that all the advances in development of the public library system in Ireland would be undone.

Equally prominent and influential in the early years of the Library Association, Fr Brown seems to have blocked any public reference to the Mayo state of affairs. Reading between the lines, it would appear that there was some dissension amongst the council of the LAI on what approach to take to the Miss Dunbar Harrison situation. Yet the council did not seem to have much of a problem taking a public stance on the admittedly less contentious Leitrim circumstance.

The carefully chosen three-person deputation from the Library Association met with the Local Appointments Commissioners on 24 February 1931. Tom Gay reported back to the executive board. Nothing came of it. The LAI published no details of this meeting and there seems to have been no further discussion of the Mayo situation at board level.

The Library Association's report, dated October 1928–April 1929, had stated that, among other aims, the organisation was founded 'to provide a pivot round which all library interests should revolve, a centre at which professional problems could be discussed and competently solved, and a vantage ground from which a sound and suitable policy would be advanced.'[33] If the LAI discussed the Mayo controversy they did so only in private. It is one of the ironies of the situation that the chairman of the LAI executive board, Tom Gay, penned the above statement.

A stalemate had developed within the Library Association so no clear stance could be taken. The most high-profile dispute involving libraries and librarianship passed by without the very organisation that represented professional librarians speaking out on it. One could argue that the Library Association had ducked its first big challenge, either from a lack of unity or a lack of nerve.

Chapter 16

'The brass-hat boyos'

The *Catholic Bulletin*, never a journal to shy away from the possibility of a conspiracy theory, had strong views on the activities of the Local Appointments Commission and did not refrain from voicing them. 'The commissioners,' it wrote, 'as is known, have a well-equipped office. One prominent personage therein, a Catholic, has openly taken his position. A son in Trinity College is a hostage to the new ascendancy … The unfortunate "board of selection" is really to be pitied. All these boards are known to be blinkered by the "brass-hat boyos" who first select them, then run them in blinkers and finally arrange "results" with chronic disregard of the recommendations of these truly pitiable "selection boards".'[1] The *Catholic Bulletin* was of the opinion that the 'Free State is a happy hunting ground for pension or job-seeking masons.'[2]

Christina Keogh, James Montgomery, Tom Gay and the other members of the Local Appointments Commission's selection board were, by any standards, respectable members of society and pillars of the community, serious and committed public and civil servants. It seems unlikely, given their background, that any accusations of partiality aimed at the interview board could hold true. This, of course, did not stop interested parties from making such allegations.

The ironic effect of the attacks on the LAC, such as those by the *Catholic Bulletin*, was that it made the Cumann na nGaedheal government more determined than ever to defend not only Letitia Dunbar Harrison but also the LAC and all of its mechanisms. Cumann na nGaedheal had emphasised all along that the LAC was not an extension of the government but a stand-alone body. In its efforts to protect the LAC, the government went to extraordinary lengths and, in the process, compromised the very reputation for independence and confidentiality they had sought to protect.

In a Dáil debate in 1928, Minister Ernest Blythe had outlined the guarantees of confidentiality that members of selection boards had been given. 'Further, people who have acted in selection boards,' he said, 'have been given an assurance that their reports would be treated confidentially. They were given a guarantee in the following terms – All communications and information which the members of the board receive as such are to be regarded as strictly confidential and the commissioners will so regard any reports or information which a board forwards to them.'[3]

The attorney general, John A. Costello, had already given his opinion that the LAC was neither independent of the Dáil nor of the executive council. While the executive council was not entitled to control the manner in which it carried out its duties, it was entitled to obtain any information that it thought proper in order to ascertain that the Commission was carrying out these duties in a proper manner.[4] Ellen Burke, by calling into question the board's decision, had set in motion this chain of events. In order to defend the LAC, President Cosgrave required them to furnish him with as much information as possible.

The state papers contain documents that reveal not only the marking scheme used by the selection board but also the actual marks received by some of the candidates. Ellen Burke was the only unsuccessful candidate whose marks were publicly aired. Regardless of the rights and wrongs of Miss Burke's allegations, having the result of her interview revealed in this way can only be described as a breach of confidentiality. Presumably, the government felt justified in doing so because Miss Burke had been the one to go public first.

The *Catholic Bulletin*, in particular, published detailed attacks on the LAC and its procedures in the recruitment process for the post of librarian in Mayo. Every deviation from accepted practice was seen as part of a conspiracy theory or a fiendish plot to foist a Protestant librarian on Catholic Mayo. The *Bulletin's* January 1931 edition listed twenty queries that they directed not at President Cosgrave, but at the so-called 'brass-hat boyos' that the paper alleged were running the LAC.

Among the questions which the *Catholic Bulletin* raised, was who had devised the conditions with regard to age, qualifications and experience for these appointments? And had these conditions been altered? The *Bulletin* alleged that there was an 'aggressive ascendancy' that was particularly concerned with medical and library appointments, two sensitive areas 'affecting the morality of the Irish people'. 'The Protestant ascendancy,' it wrote, 'will continue in being, with all its assumptions of superiority, as arrogant as they are unfounded, and with all its venomous purposes of imposing its alien thought, its special standards of moral conduct, standards now publicly and palpably debased, on the Catholic people of this country.'[5] This was the basis of the *Bulletin's* conspiracy theories, though the insertion of a Protestant in the library service of County Mayo does seem like a somewhat convoluted way of undermining Catholicism in Ireland. However, there were questions to answer. There was enough uncertainty surrounding the activities of the LAC to raise some doubts about the selection of Letitia Dunbar Harrison.

– Miss Dunbar Harrison was not yet twenty-five.

– Miss Dunbar Harrison did not have a library qualification.

– In the first advertisement for the post Irish was listed as an essential requirement. In the second, this was relaxed.

The LAC had an answer for each of these questions. In cases such as this, work experience could be counted to make up the required age. This was custom and practice at the time. The advertisement had stated that a library qualification was desirable rather than essential. President Cosgrave had explained in the Dáil that the reason the Irish language requirement had been relaxed was because of the difficulty in recruiting experienced librarians with the requisite competence in the language. Miss Dunbar Harrison would have three years to reach the desired standard. As county librarians worked alone in many of these newly set-up organisations, it was felt that practical experience was more relevant than an academic qualification. There was a certain ambiguity as to what counted as practical experience. The Library Association of Ireland had received a letter from a different unsuccessful candidate, Miss Kerrigan, asking for clarification of what exactly the LAC meant by 'library experience'.[6] In his letters to the press, Canon Hegarty had also questioned this procedure. Was it service in a library that counted as 'experience' or was it service as a librarian?

'Vouched expenses of locomotion'

It is perhaps instructive to look at the job description and conditions of employment for the Mayo post.

The Conditions of Appointment
County Librarian – Mayo

1. The post is whole-time, permanent and pensionable.
2. Salary £250 per annum with vouched expenses of locomotion when travelling on official duty.
3. Applicants must be not less than twenty-five nor more than forty years of age on 1 May 1930, with the provision that actual service as librarian not exceeding two years may be added to bring a candidate's age to the minimum limit of twenty-five years.
4. Duties of county librarian: – To act as secretary to the county library committee, to check and keep all accounts, to compile lists of books for submission to the book-selection committee, to attend all meetings of the committee and other meetings at which the library scheme may come under review, to prepare reports and be responsible to the committee for the proper management and supervision of the scheme throughout the county, to superintend the staff of the county book repository and generally to advise and help towards development of the scheme by promotion of lectures

and such other duties as may from time to time be assigned by the committee.

5. Essential qualifications: – (a) Good general education, (b) Training in or experience of library work. A diploma in library training and practical experience in office organisation are desirable qualifications.

6. A substantial preference will be given to qualified candidates with a competent knowledge of Irish. If no qualified candidate with a competent knowledge of Irish be available the successful candidate will be required to comply with the terms of the Local Offices and Employments (Gaeltacht) Order, 1928.

7. Preference will be given to those who have had experience in the organisation and management of public libraries.

8. The person appointed will be required to enter into a fidelity guarantee bond of £200 as security for the proper discharge of the duties of the post.

9. In the event of a female officer being appointed resignation on marriage will be compulsory.[7]

The ninth condition is the infamous 'marriage bar' which survived in Ireland up to the 1970s. It goes without saying that this ultra discriminatory policy would be illegal modern Ireland.

'Women who love it more than marriage'

Librarianship was one profession in which it was socially acceptable for women to show an interest. In the 1935 report on public library provision in the Irish Free State, of the twenty-four county librarians listed, half were female. In an interview with Maura Laverty in 1930, headlined 'Taking Charge of a Library – Women Who Love it More than Marriage', Roísín Walsh, Dublin city's librarian, explained, 'Almost without exception the women who dedicate themselves to library work grow to love it so much that they can rarely forsake it – even for the attraction of married life. Seriously though, I have yet to meet the woman librarian who does not find her work utterly fascinating and engrossing.'[8] In the same article Maura Laverty made the claim that Roísín Walsh, city librarian-elect of Dublin, was the first woman in Europe to attain such a position.

There were ways around the marriage bar. In 1936 Kathleen White resigned from her post as county librarian of Leitrim in order to get married and was replaced by Vera Carey. Four years later Vera Carey herself was about to be married and submitted her resignation as required. Her brother happened to be a solicitor and like all good solicitors he found a loophole in the legislation. While she was required to resign upon marrying there was no impediment to her being re-employed. Having discovered that there was no bar on it Vera McCarthy, as she was by then known, promptly re-applied for her old job and was re-appointed.[9]

There was a good deal of conflict at this turn of events in Leitrim. 'At national level, there was the embarrassment that a loophole in the legislation had been discovered and a flurry of activity to stop this happening again.' At a local level there was yet another heated debate as there was support for an alternative, local candidate.[10] Libraries and controversy seemed to go hand-in-hand when it came to Leitrim in the 1920s and 1930s.

The headings under which the interview board assigned their marks were as follows:

- General Education
- Professional Qualifications
- Practical Library Experience
- Special Experience
- Personality
- Irish

Irish was marked separately to the other categories, with either a pass or a fail grade being assigned. The category 'Special Experience' covered such areas as familiarity with the county library service, knowledge of rural Ireland and also of office organisation.

The following is a comparison of the marks received by Miss Dunbar Harrison and Miss Burke:

	Miss Dunbar Harrison	*Miss Burke*
General Education (100)	80	65
Professional Qualifications (150)	0	100
Practical Library Experience (100)	50	10
Special Experience (150)	40	0
Personality (200)	150	75
Total (700)	320	250

Both women failed the Irish test. The pass standard was set at 75 per cent. Ellen Burke fared slightly better with 40 per cent while Letitia Dunbar Harrison received 20 per cent.[11] So, according to these figures Miss Dunbar Harrison prevailed due to her personality, her experience and her education. The lack of any professional qualification did not prove to be a handicap. The selection board seemed to be more impressed by practical know-how than academic achievements. There is, of course, a discrepancy in that they were interviewed at different times by a slightly altered interview board: Miss Dunbar Harrison on 4 April 1930, Miss Burke on 12 July 1930. The original chairman, James Montgomery, had not been available on the second date 'owing to an urgent business call'.[12] The Commission also passed on the information that, at a later date, Ellen Burke applied for the post of county librarian in Clare. Having gone before a different interview board she was again unsuccessful. This post went to Dermot Foley.

The commission also released Miss Burke's marks on this occasion, emphasising that she had gone before the board as No. 6, i.e. they did not know who she was. The Commission was anxious to make the point that even though the Clare interview took place after Ellen Burke's name had entered the public domain with regard to the Mayo controversy, she would not have been discriminated against as this board would not have known her name. Nevertheless, Miss Burke must have felt under a great deal of pressure. Her marks for personality declined from 75 out of 150 the first time to 40 out of 200 at the second interview. She also failed the Irish test a second time, again receiving 40 per cent. Her marks this time were as follows:

General Education (100)	70
Professional Qualifications (150)	100
Practical Library Experience (100)	10
Special Experience (150)	10
Personality (200)	40
Total (700)	230

The doubts cast on Miss Dunbar Harrison, as to her age, experience, lack of qualifications and her inability to speak Irish, had all been answered by President Cosgrave. The political problem facing him was that while he could answer each of these accusations, he could not win over those of a paranoid disposition, who were convinced that a conspiracy was afoot. Some of the mud being flung was bound to stick.

The situation was one of stalemate. Six months had passed and there was still no sign of a solution. Commissioner Bartley administered the day-to-day business of the county, meeting with a certain amount of resistance. Letitia Dunbar Harrison worked away as librarian in the courthouse in Castlebar while the vast majority of the population of Mayo refused to have anything to do with the libraries she was running. However, after six months of relative quiet all of a sudden the controversy flared back into life.

'A first-class political crisis'

On 17 June 1931 the political correspondent of the *Irish Independent* reported that 'the circumstances surrounding the abolition of the Mayo County Council and the appointment of Miss Dunbar Harrison as librarian threaten to bring about the defeat of the government to-day, and to create a first-class political crisis.

'The central figure in a situation which developed over the week-end with almost dramatic suddenness is Mr Michael Davis, chairman of the government party in the Dáil and chairman of the Mayo County Council. Very quietly ... and without consulting any of his colleagues he handed in ... a motion: That the Dáil declines to give a second reading of the Local Government Bill, which includes as one of its provisions a proposal to extend the power of the Minister for Local Government and public health in relation to local authorities dissolved by him until the minister takes the necessary steps to restore the Mayo County Council. The government takes a very serious view of the motion and it was specially considered by the cabinet ...'

Michael Davis was called in for a special meeting with President Cosgrave and Richard Mulcahy but he was determined to hold his ground. He told the *Irish Independent* that as chairman of Mayo County Council, he felt very keenly the action of the minister in suppressing it. 'I could not,' he said, 'allow the opportunity which this bill presents to pass without bringing the matter up.' He regretted that circumstances should have arisen which compelled him to take this course. The Local Government Bill, 1931, set out to strengthen the power of the Minister for Local Government, enabling him to more easily dissolve county councils. The danger for the government, as the independent put it, was that on a vote, Michael Davis was 'almost certain to take with him into the division lobby against the government two members of the government party for Mayo – Messrs M. Nally and M. Henry.'[13]

The Irish Times reported that 'a piquant situation' had arisen. 'Deputies of all parties,' it wrote, 'were greatly intrigued at the situation ... The probable explanation is that the government deputies from County Mayo have found it necessary, owing to local pressure, to have the question debated in the Dáil.'[14] *The Irish Times* added that the two Fianna Fáil TDs, P.J. Ruttledge and Richard

Walsh, had had a motion on the order paper for some time, but hadn't had the opportunity to move it.

> That the Dáil disapproves of the action of the Minister for Local Government and public health in dissolving the Mayo County Council, and demands its immediate restoration.

Was this a minor mutiny or would he gain the support of other TDs from the government's backbenches? It was rumoured that other west of Ireland backbenchers might vote against the government. The *Irish Independent* calculated that, allowing for members who were ill, the government could be beaten by one or two votes. If other Cumann na nGaedheal deputies joined the revolt and Davis was successful with his amendment, it could bring down the government.

Chapter 17

'A weakling and a wobbler'

At long last the Mayo library controversy was going to be the subject of a debate in the Dáil chambers. On 17 June, Richard Mulcahy moved the second reading of the Local Government Bill, 1931. Michael Davis then proposed his amendment, opposing the bill on the grounds that the minister should not be given any more authority until such time as Mayo County Council was restored. He outlined the background to his decision to rebel against his own party.

'I think it will be within the knowledge of every member of the house,' he said, 'if not within the knowledge of every individual in the Free State, that the position of Mayo County Council loomed very much in the limelight in the not-too-distant past, and I think I might place on the shoulders of the Minister for Local Government the sole responsibility for putting the Mayo County Council out of office.'[1]

Deputy Davis went on to summarise the series of events that had led to the installation of Miss Dunbar Harrison as librarian. He argued that Irish had been required. 'The Mayo County Council was dissolved,' he declared, 'not, I am in a position to claim, for inefficiency.' He explained that the inspector sent down by the minister to investigate the state of affairs had only spent fifteen minutes at the sworn inquiry.

'There was no question of anything being wrong,' he said, 'it was a question of the disobedience of the council.'

Mulcahy seemed surprised at the brevity if not the tone of Michael Davis' comments. 'Am I to understand,' he enquired, 'that that is all the criticism that there is on the matter?'

The Ceann Comhairle then opened the debate on the amendment. P.J. Ruttledge, a Fianna Fáil TD from Mayo, expressed disbelief and cynicism as to the motives behind the actions of Deputy Davis, claiming that he himself had in fact submitted a virtually identical amendment to the Ceann Comhairle.

'I would declare the amendment,' he said, 'as a pretence or a sham attempt to throw dust in the eyes of the people of Mayo and at the same time to let the minister out of a difficulty. Here we have as a result of this collusion between the minister and Deputy Davis, this amendment tabled and we have the newspapers this morning scheduling it and portraying it in double-column headings as a first-class situation.'[2]

Deputy Ruttledge went on to query some of the procedures used by the Local Appointments Commission in its selection of Miss Dunbar Harrison, in particular the raising of the recruitment age. He questioned the fact that 'the lady appointed got more marks for "personality" than the others got … People who want to do it, and people who did do it, got that vague word "personality" to cover a multitude of the sins they may commit … but personality would be of very little use to Irish speakers in Mayo …'

He then spoke of the religious issue, closely echoing the words and opinions of Dean D'Alton and Canon Hegarty at the library committee meeting. 'There is one matter that I have to speak about,' he said, 'and I do it with considerable reluctance, for the reason that when you speak about these matters you are often likely to be misunderstood.' Deputy Ruttledge denied any sectarian bias but insisted that a 99 per cent Catholic county like Mayo was entitled to have a Catholic librarian. In this he reaffirmed the words of his party's leader, Eamon de Valera, at the public meeting in Irishtown, County Mayo, in January 1931. He outlined the series of events that had led to the dissolution of the council, paying particular attention to the role of Michael Davis as chairman of the council and as senior Cumann na nGaedheal TD for the county.

'I know what happened subsequently when Deputy Davis came up to Dublin,' he said, 'when he was accused by the minister of being "a weakling and a wobbler".'

'Will I have the right of reply to this?' asked Deputy Davis.

'No,' replied the Ceann Comhairle.

'I am very sorry ...' persisted Deputy Davis.

'Hold a meeting when you go home,' suggested Deputy Killilea.

'... in Crossmolina,' added Richard Mulcahy.

'Yes,' agreed Deputy Ruttledge. 'Crossmolina seems to be the place where we all hold them – both sides.'

'Let us keep to the debate here,' advised the Ceann Comhairle, 'and not stray to the crossroads.'[3]

Ruttledge continued, accusing the minister of suppressing the council and misleading the senate when he had answered questions there on 25 March 1931.

'Gracious me!' exclaimed Mulcahy.

'What is the good gracious about?' protested Deputy Ruttledge.

'The minister will get his opportunity,' interjected the Ceann Comhairle.

'If we could get more good graces in Mayo we would be better off,' murmured Deputy Ruttledge. He went on to outline the state of the library service in Mayo since the appointment of Letitia Dunbar Harrison, revealing that the vast majority of the library centres had returned their books by March 1931. He had tried in vain to get more up-to-date information.

'I believe he visits Mayo occasionally'

'I understand the Commissioner [P.J. Bartley] might be away. I believe he visits Mayo occasionally,' continued Deputy Ruttledge dryly. 'There are books with about thirty of the 112 library centres ... The fact is that only four centres are in semi-operation out of 112 in operation since last December, when the minister started this heavy hand. The people who patronise these four centres which are in semi-operation are people of a religious persuasion which is the opposite to the majority of the people of Mayo.'[4]

Deputy Ruttledge then brought up the difficulties faced by the various committees of Mayo County Council. Commissioner Bartley was unable to take over the duties of the Old Age Pensions Committee or the Technical Instruction Committee. From the time of his appointment technical instructors had not, and could not, be paid.

'Perhaps the minister hoped the people of Mayo would reel under his feet,' continued Deputy Ruttledge, 'that they would come forward and appoint committees to assist the commissioner he had sent down. He may hope as long as he likes. Until he removes the person appointed from that position, and removes the Commissioner from the office he has been appointed to as a result of refusing to appoint this lady, he may rest assured that there is no hope whatever that the priests and people are going to crumble under his feet.

'He may be keen on dictatorship, and he may think that the people are going to give way after a time. The people of Mayo are united on this issue; they are more united than ever they have been in the history of that county before, and no attempt by the minister to trample on them, and import amongst them a person in the position of librarian who they have good reason to believe may prove a danger to the faith of the people, will succeed. They are not going to let the minister walk on them.'

Dick Walsh, also a Fianna Fáil TD for Mayo, endorsed the arguments of Deputy Ruttledge. The Vocational Education Act was 'a dead letter' in Mayo due to the impasse created in the county by the actions of the minister.

'He can get no man in Mayo,' Dick Walsh declared, 'either clergyman or public man or any responsible person, to act upon the Vocational Education Committee or any committee connected with local affairs … There may be places in the County Mayo where, as a result of these vacancies remaining unfilled, people cannot get their old-age pensions.'

Deputy Walsh went on to re-iterate his stance on the issue. 'When this question came up in the Mayo County Council,' he said, 'I myself clearly indicated that we who are members of the Fianna Fáil Party in the council were not actuated by any question of bigotry, that we were not influenced by what I might call anti-Protestantism, that we did not object to Protestants or other non-Catholics in this country getting their share of public appointments.'

Deputy Walsh criticised *The Irish Times* for trying to portray Fianna Fáil as intolerant because of the actions of their councillors in Mayo. 'We are not a party of bigots,' he said. 'But neither I nor any member of Fianna Fáil in the County Mayo or in this Dáil apologise to anybody for being Catholics or for taking up a Catholic attitude on a question of vital importance to Catholic interests. If the minister thinks he is going to cow the people and the priests of Mayo in this matter, he is making a great mistake. If he thinks he is going to gain political kudos by proving to a certain element in this country that his is the great party of tolerance; if he thinks that by creeping to certain elements in this country who are always anti-national and anti-Catholic that he is going to gain anything, and that he is going to increase prestige of his party west of the Shannon, he is certainly making a great mistake.'[5]

Deputy Walsh referred to the history of Mayo and its 'very bitter memories ... A large number of the small farmers of the county have not very sweet memories of those times, times when they were faced with the alternative of the roadside or of changing their religion.' He argued that the minister risked intensifying the tension and bitterness between neighbours in Mayo because of his actions. Mayo County Council had been abolished for what was only a technical breach. The inspector sent down had given the council a clean bill of health after a sworn inquiry that lasted barely fifteen minutes. Deputy Walsh then proceeded to criticise Deputy T.J. O'Connell, the leader of the Labour Party and also a Mayo TD, for not condemning Commissioner Bartley for reducing the wages of the road workers in Mayo from thirty-five shillings to thirty-two shillings a week.

'It could happen, and you not hear it,' protested Deputy O'Connell.

'A long way of using a short word'

Deputy Walsh then accused Richard Mulcahy of making 'a deliberate misstatement' in the chamber. The Ceann Comhairle intervened. 'The deputy ought not to accuse the minister,' he said, 'or any other deputy of making a deliberate misstatement. That is a long way of using a short word. The deputy can say if he wishes that the minister was wrong in his statement.'

'It can stand as far as I am concerned,' declared Richard Mulcahy.

Walsh went on to criticise Trinity College, despite the objections of the acting Ceann Comhairle, Mr F. Fahy, who had taken over the chair.

'The deputy should leave Trinity College alone,' insisted Mr Fahy. 'Trinity College is not one of the bodies dissolved.'

Nevertheless, Professor William Thrift rose to defend Trinity. Some mud slinging resulted until the acting Ceann Comhairle finally put a stop to it. 'This is neither the time nor the place,' he said.

'A little manliness'

Deputy Michael Clery congratulated Michael Davis on his courage. 'I am glad as a Mayo deputy,' he said, 'that the day has come in this house when there is a question on which Deputy Davis and myself can stand shoulder to shoulder. I certainly am glad of the attitude he has taken on this question. Deputy Davis has proved to have a little manliness in him. It is about time.'[6]

Deputy Clery alleged that the crisis had arisen at that particular time because of the imminent South Dublin by-election. 'The instructions to have that appointment insisted upon,' he said, 'came to the minister from the Orange Lodges of County Dublin … and also to the instructions of *The Irish Times* … At the time he found it was politic to flout the people of Mayo, to flout the wishes of the clergy there, and to dance instead in attendance on the unionists and masons of the County Dublin, whose votes did count at the time for the minister and his party.'

Deputy Clery outlined his views regarding Richard Mulcahy's personality. 'There was a time in the past,' he said, 'when this self-opinionated minister, this over-rider of the people's rights, got out of his opponents in another fashion. There was a time when not abolition but execution was his method of putting his opponents aside. Now since he finds he can put them aside in another way, according to law, his method is not execution, but abolition … He believes if he had been born in this country six generations ago, this country would be a little heaven now. I believe the minister means well.'

'It will be alright in six generations,' commented Richard Mulcahy.

'I believe he means well,' repeated Deputy Clery, 'but he cannot convince me he is right and 99 per cent of the people are wrong.'[7]

Deputy T.J. O'Connell rose next. 'Of the nine deputies who represent Mayo,' he said, 'six are members of the county council and I was awaiting until these men, who are more closely associated with the matter than I, would have spoken.' Deputy O'Connell concentrated his argument on his unhappiness with the methodology that the Local Appointments Commission interview board had used. He did not address the issue of Miss Dunbar Harrison's selection directly. The Local Appointments Commission had not advertised the various county library vacancies separately nor had they held separate interviews for those different posts. In his opinion this invalidated the process and justified the council's rejection of Miss Dunbar Harrison. He also took the opportunity to defend himself against Deputy Walsh's accusation that he had done nothing in regard to the reduction in the wages of Mayo's road workers.

'A statement was made that I,' he said, 'as a Mayo representative, did not take any action or as the deputy said, that he did not hear that I took any action. A great many things happen about which the deputy does not hear. I have here in front of me a file of correspondence showing that so far back as the first week in April I took action in the matter.'

Deputy Hugo Flinn congratulated the backbenchers of the Cumann na nGaedheal Party. 'While I do not wish in any way to be personal,' he said, 'I do say that it is a very useful and a very hopeful sign, perhaps the first sign in the darkness, which we have seen for a very long time – the darkness of the backbenchers of Cumann na nGaedheal – that there is still somewhere amongst them some backbone, some remaining element of those qualities which made a man walk erect instead of creeping on his belly like a worm.'

Deputy Flinn drew attention to the fact that Michael Davis was a vice-chairman of his party and was opposing his own minister. He concluded that all nine Mayo TDs were as one on this issue and stated that Mayo was united, preferring to see their County Council abolished, rather than to have something imposed on them by a central authority.

'Unless we have to assume that he is a superman, unless we are prepared to assume that some special inspiration from heaven has given him the wisdom which enables him to know in relation to this County Council more than Cumann na nGaedheal, more than Fianna Fáil, more than Labour, more than priests and people know about it, we must assume he is a superman of a different character, a man whose sole supermanship is in the claim to override the organised, united, public opinion of a county on a matter of which they have full and complete knowledge.'

He went on to express two possible justifications for this attitude. 'One explanation,' he said, 'is that the minister does actually believe himself to be the legitimate over-rider of the people, that he has a malignant opposition to the rights of the people to express an effective opinion in relation to their own local government. That is one explanation. The other is downright stupidity. I think it is downright stupidity at the back of all this ... He had to break the County Council rather than his own pride.'[8]

Deputy Seán T. O'Kelly was also highly critical of Richard Mulcahy, 'the would-be Napoleon, the pocket battleship, the pocket dreadnought of the Free State, that fears nothing.' He read into the Dáil minutes details of the December meeting of Mayo library committee.

President Cosgrave rose to make a robust defence of Richard Mulcahy. He may not have had anything new to say on the matter but he seemed determined to show his support for his beleaguered Minister for Local Government. He made reference to the *Catholic Bulletin*, in particular the list of questions it had published in its January 1931 issue. President Cosgrave claimed, 'I have not read that paper since it committed what was to my mind a very serious mistake against Christianity; that was a criticism of the late General Collins after his death.'

'Glory be to God,' replied Deputy O'Kelly. 'If that be want of Christianity I hope the President will examine his own conscience.'

'I do,' said Cosgrave, 'very often.'[9]

Deputy O'Kelly suggested a solution to the impasse. 'An effort should be made to get Miss Dunbar married to some eligible member of the County Council,' he said, 'and thereby get her out of an awkward position and the government out of its present mess ... I wonder will the president look round the county and see if there is any eligible young fellow who might get him out of a scrape, for at present he is in a bad way?'

President Cosgrave stood by Richard Mulcahy and the Local

Appointments Commission, taking the debate through the various measures that had led to the installation of Miss Dunbar Harrison as Mayo county librarian.

'What about the president's own party?' asked Deputy Clery. 'The chairman of the party introduced this motion.' 'I did not interrupt the deputy when he was speaking,' replied the president, 'and he spoke at great length. I believe he invited members of this party to go into the division lobby along with him. They know what to do, but they will not be attracted by that sort of clap-trap.'

'You never know,' replied Clery.[10]

Deputy Eamon de Valera intervened, squandering much time and energy in a squabble with the Ceann Comhairle over standing orders and procedural matters, the withdrawal of the Fianna Fáil amendment and the allowing of a similarly worded amendment from Deputy Davis. The Ceann Comhairle denied any bias and stated that he had merely been trying to be helpful, expediting the business of the house. Deputy de Valera eventually came round to the substance of the debate. In the first place, he was against the appointment of Miss Dunbar Harrison because he fundamentally disagreed with centralisation. Then there was the matter of religion. 'I say that if I had a vote on a local body,' he said, 'and if there were two qualified people who had to deal with a Catholic community, and if one was a Catholic and the other a Protestant, I would unhesitatingly vote for the Catholic. Let us be clear and let us know where we are.'

He went on to argue that libraries should be treated similarly to schools. 'If this librarian were simply a sort of clerk,' he said, 'who attended to somebody who came in and handed out a book which that person asked for, then I would not have any hesitation in saying that it was not an educational position, and that there was no reason whatever for introducing religion in that case. The more, however, I examine the question, the more I satisfy myself that if the library system were meant to achieve anything, it should be an educational system, and that the work of the librarian should be actively to interest people in reading books, and that it should not be a mere passive position simply of handing down books.

'I say if it is a mere passive position of handing down books that are asked for, then the librarian has no particular duty for which religion should be regarded as a qualification, but if the librarian goes round to the homes of the people trying to interest them in books, sees the children in the schools and asks these children to bring home certain books, or asks what books their parents would like to read; if it is active work of a propagandist educational character – and I believe it must be such if it is to be of any value at all and worth the money spent on it – then I say the people of Mayo, in a county where, I think – I forget the figures – over 98 per cent of the population is Catholic, are justified in insisting upon a Catholic librarian …

'If the library system is an educational system, the same freedom should be accorded, and whatever is necessary to give the Protestant community their facilities, then it should be provided, but do not try to meet the difficulty in such a way as you are doing in Mayo.'[11]

Deputy Thomas Mullins, an independent republican, pointed out the irony that the Minister for Local Government was also chairman of the Gaeltacht Commission which had been set up to investigate how best to preserve the Irish language. He condemned Richard Mulcahy as 'one who out-Neros Nero. And who is more dictatorial than the Spanish Inquisition, presiding over the Department of Local Government, telling the people of Mayo – remember they are only bog-men and do not matter – to accept his instructions or to get out. Be it said to the credit of Mayo County Council they did get out rather than bend the knee.'

Deputy Mullins was particularly critical of the religious, sectarian attitude introduced by some deputies. 'There is plenty of material to damn the minister,' he said, 'and to crucify him fifteen times over, without introducing any other aspect.' However, despite his reservations Deputy Mullins was still in favour of the amendment.

'Corrupt in twopence-halfpenny matters'

Deputy Frank Aiken argued that in the old days 'it was said that local bodies were corrupt in twopence-halfpenny matters. But these are the gentlemen who are corrupt in matters of hundreds and thousands of pounds.'[12]

As the debate was nearing its end, Richard Mulcahy made his defence at length. He defended the actions of his department. 'We might have mandamused the council,' he said, 'and got an order from the court that the Mayo County Council should so act. We did not do so for the reason that in the final minutes of the Mayo County Council dealing with the matter they instructed their solicitor to take the fullest possible steps to resist the mandamus and they decided that they would defer until their next meeting what they would do about striking a library rate. There was no reason in the first place why the rate-payers of Mayo should be saddled with the cost of mandamus proceedings and there was no reason in my opinion why I, as representing this assembly, should allow the Mayo County Council to put us in the position that they had to evade their statutory duties by declining to provide the necessary funds for the carrying on of the library.'

Mulcahy was particularly critical of Deputy de Valera's remarks. 'I say that the deputy has gone as near saying as constitutionally he can, that no Protestant librarian should be appointed to county libraries in this country.'

He also mentioned that there had been Protestant librarians working in the Free State. 'I do not think that you can have one religious policy in Mayo and another in Leix,' he said. 'I am in the position as Minister for Local Government of having an official document giving the greatest possible praise to a Protestant county librarian in one county and condemning the idea of having a Protestant as librarian in another county ... I have nothing to show me that a Protestant librarian can be a danger to faith more or less in Mayo, but not in some other county. As an ordinary lay

Irishman, I deny that County Mayo is any more Catholic than my own native county or any other county.'

As he neared the conclusion of his defence, Richard Mulcahy raised the issue of finance, criticising Mayo County Council's expenditure and in effect telling the people of Mayo that they were better off with a commissioner controlling the purse strings. 'I believe the people of Mayo,' he said, 'are people who pay their rates pretty well up to date, and the people of Mayo who responded to a demand from the County Council in the year 1928-29 by giving them £71,000 odd to carry on their administration had to respond two years afterwards, in the year 1930-31, by giving them an additional £51,000.'

'The minister is attacking his own party on the council,' protested Deputy Walsh.

'I am being attacked by my own party,' replied Minister Mulcahy.

'He is now attacking them.'

'I am telling my own party that it might not be a bad day's work done on the ordinary administration side.'

'Let him test public opinion and he will know it,' added Deputy Walsh.

'There was just one other point which I might answer,' continued Richard Mulcahy. 'Deputy Walsh is full of talk here.'

'He wants your job,' suggested Deputy Sheehy from Cork by way of explanation.

'He gets more coherent when he goes down to Mayo,' alleged Mulcahy, 'and you get somehow to understand him better when he speaks from a platform in Mayo, as reported in some of the local papers, than you do when hearing him here on certain matters. I think the same might be said of Deputy Clery and Deputy Ruttledge.'

'Crusaders,' exclaimed Deputy Gorey.

'Deputy Gorey is more at home with his bulls in Kilkenny,' jeered Mr Kennedy.

'We are told that we would not have stood by the law in County Mayo were it not that there was a Dublin by-election on, that the freemasons dictated to us – that we had to stand by the appointment of this lady, and that we knuckled under to the freemasons because there was a by-election in County Dublin,' concluded Richard Mulcahy. He then proceeded to go into forensic detail with regard to his party's electoral support in County Dublin and argued that they had no need for any extra votes there. Their candidate had received 35,362 votes as opposed to 15,024 for the Fianna Fáil candidate. 'Deputies on the opposite side ought to read their own papers,' he advised, 'Catholic journalism to be effective and to be truly Catholic needs first of all to be fair. We have comments from the great Catholic party over there who are going to replace the bishops in telling us …'

'No, no; it is the minister who is going to replace the bishops in the west of Ireland,' interrupted Deputy Walsh.

Richard Mulcahy continued: 'that in the matter of doctors and librarians we should be fair. They have to answer, not only to the people here and to one another, but they have to answer some place else for the methods they employ to try to establish the Kingdom of God here on earth.'

The Dáil was divided: Tá, 73; Níl, 62. The Mayo deputies, Michael Davis and Mark Henry, sided against their party, but were not joined by any of their Cumann na nGaedheal colleagues. The Farmers' Party and the independent deputies in the main, voted against the amendment. It was solidly supported by Fianna Fáil and the Labour Party. Deputy Fitzgerald-Kenney, the Minister for Justice, was the only Mayo TD to support the government.

The government had prevailed. Later, at that same sitting of the Dáil, Deputy Ruttledge's long-delayed motion on the dissolution of Mayo County Council was put forward. 'That the Dáil disapproves of the action of the Minister for Local Government and public health in dissolving the Mayo County Council, and demands its immediate restoration.' As this substantive matter had already been dealt with, this was voted on without debate. The Dáil divided on this occasion: Tá, 60; Níl, 73. Deputy Michael Davis abstained.

'The pangs of intellectual famine'

The Irish Times labelled the Dáil debate 'The Battle of the Books'. 'Mr Davis,' it wrote, 'from whom we cannot withhold our sympathy, was torn between two loyalties. He is not merely a member of the government party, but is a chairman of that party in the Dáil. On the other hand, he was chairman of the dissolved County Council, and we may assume that the local pressure which compelled him thus to challenge his own government and, perhaps to endanger its very existence, was exceedingly strong. He must have known that all the government's opponents in the house would rally joyfully to his amendment. Fortunately, the debate and its result not only have not impaired the government's position, but have strengthened it. Mr Davis' amendment has been defeated by seventy-three votes to sixty-two – a quite substantial majority for the cause of political and religious tolerance.'

The Irish Times went on to concede that 'the only case for the amendment was that County Mayo is now enduring the pangs of intellectual famine. Its library service is virtually at a standstill, and the books from more than one hundred rural centres are lying idle at Castlebar. This is a sad state of things and its continuance will do harm; but infinitely greater harm would have been done by the Dáil's refusal to support the government's liberal and enlightened policy.'[13]

In conclusion *The Irish Times* wrote that 'the Dáil's acceptance of Mr Davis' amendment would have been an invitation to administrative chaos; for every public body that Mr Mulcahy has been forced to suppress or correct would have hastened to challenge him in parliament.'[14]

The Times of London was by now taking an interest. 'Although the republican party [Fianna Fáil],' it wrote, 'have occasionally paid lip-service to the principles of religious toleration, they, nonetheless, took up the cudgels for the Mayo County Council, and attacked not only the "horrid arbitrariness" of the minister but also the appointment of a Protestant to a post in a Roman Catholic country.' The paper went on to claim that if Mr de Valera should win the next election that, 'Protestants may be promised equality of opportunity, but are likely to be effectively debarred from public service in the Irish Free State.'[15]

The *Catholic Bulletin*, predictably enough, was not impressed. 'The stage management,' it wrote, 'of the three days that preceded the Mayo library and County Council debate held by Mr Mulcahy as dictator and general on Wednesday, 17 June, would be no credit even to a minor travelling circus. Mr Davis, chairman of the Cosgrave Party Machine, had been remarkably quiet all through the past six months … that the Davis motion was a palpable frame-up, to afford a would-be dictator an opportunity of whitewashing himself is but too obvious.'[16]

The following day a meeting of the Cumann na nGaedheal parliamentary party discussed the matter but, following a statement by Michael Davis and a short debate, decided not to take action against him and he remained in his position as chairman of the party. This would lead one to believe that his own party leaders did not take his public act of rebellion too seriously. They condoned his action. In fact they may even have colluded in it.

Eamon de Valera's complaints to the Ceann Comhairle had some justification. He suspected that Michael Davis had put down his amendment and the government had manipulated the order of business so as to get his debate on to the floor of the Dáil in advance of Deputy Ruttledge's motion on the dissolution of Mayo Council, thereby drawing the sting out of that debate. This may only have been a bit of debating-room sharp practice but it was some form of small victory for the government.

Chapter 18

'The library crux'

The Cumann na nGaedheal government was hopeful, and not for the first time, that the political storm clouds hanging over Mayo had at long last passed. But they were to be disappointed yet again. There were some faint stirrings over Richard Mulcahy's staunch defence of his actions, but they came mainly from members of his own party. Seán Ruane was a county councillor in Mayo and had spoken at the special meeting of the council in favour of the appointment of Letitia Dunbar Harrison. He was also President of the Connacht Council of the GAA. He wrote to Richard Mulcahy expressing support for the minister's performance in the Dáil debate. He received the following reply from Richard Mulcahy:

> Many thanks for your note of the 20th [June 1931]. I will send you a copy of the official debates as soon as they are issued. The whole debate was terribly disgraceful on the side of the Mayo men. On nothing in connection with the matter had they the facts – whether as regards age or Irish or Local Appointments Commission or the relations between the library committee and the County Council. And as far as policy goes, the implications of their speeches insofar as you can get anything coherent from them on the question of policy appear more disgraceful ever still.
>
> When a week or so has passed and you can size up what the effect of the proceedings have had in Mayo generally I would be glad to have a short note telling me what you think the position in Mayo has been and whether it has eased the position (1) for Davis and (2) for us generally.[1]

There is at least an acknowledgement of Michael Davis' difficulties in his home constituency and the merest hint of sympathy for his position. This contrasted greatly with the minister's dismissive public stance of his party colleague, and would lend a certain weight to Fianna Fáil's much-trumpeted accusation that the Davis amendment that led to the Dáil debate was little more than a political charade, especially if one takes into account that the party took no punitive action against Michael Davis for his mutinous exploits.

In a private letter, Brother S.B. MacSwiney, Christian Brothers, Brow-of-the-Hill, Derry, congratulated Richard Mulcahy on 'the magnificent reply he made to attacks *re* the Mayo librarian in the Dáil last week.'[2] Generally, members of the clergy who had a previous allegiance with Cumann na nGaedheal had less of a problem with the appointment of Miss Dunbar Harrison. Canon McHugh of Claremorris was perhaps the most prominent; though he was aware he was out of step with public opinion in his county.

As the Dáil debate receded into memory there was no change in the circumstances that held sway in Mayo. Miss Dunbar Harrison's library service was still being boycotted. The various sub-committees of the County Council were still in limbo. An effective stalemate endured. As the *Connacht Sentinel* put it, 'Boycotting, which originated in Mayo during the Land War, and was successfully used in dealing with landlords and others, has now been employed with equal success in killing the government's Vocational Education Committee in that county. For the nine months ended on 1 September not one of the twenty domestic science, Irish, lace, commercial or manual instructors has been paid, simply because members of the Vocational Education Committee will not meet as a protest against the decision of the government in appointing a Protestant librarian for the county ... no pay sheets have been signed, because the act provides that five members are needed for a quorum.'[3]

Boycott was an emotive term in Mayo. As the *Sentinel* pointed out, boycotting had a long and proud history in the county, the word in fact deriving from the ostracism of Captain Charles Cunningham Boycott and his workers at Lough Mask House near Ballinrobe during the Land War. However, there is perhaps a difference between boycotting being used as a method of passive resistance by an oppressed community with little other means of protesting and a strong majority using it as a tool of oppression.

The cabinet in its initial communications with Archbishop Gilmartin of Tuam, had endeavoured to get him to sponsor a compromise by which he would persuade some of the priests of his diocese to sit on Commissioner Bartley's Vocational Education Committee, thereby allowing sanction for the payment of these teachers to be passed. While initially the archbishop had seemed willing to go along with such a deal, he later backed away from it, one suspects due to the intransigence of his priests who were unwilling to make any concession. It was perhaps a sign of how confident the priests of the county were in the strength of their position. They were in no mood to back down.

'The will of the people'

The newly established Fianna Fáil daily paper, *The Irish Press*, reported that 'since the compulsory installation of Miss Letitia Dunbar Harrison as county librarian the elaborate vocational education scheme evolved for Mayo has remained in the stocks and all the teachers appointed have not received a penny salary from the beginning of the year ... As a protest against what has been regarded as a flouting of the will of the people, eleven members of the VEC ignore the monthly notices summoning them to their meeting, and in the absence of a quorum of five no progress can be made. The two attending members are Mr P.J. Bartley, the Commissioner administering the affairs of the County Council, and the Very Reverend Canon M.J. McHugh, of Claremorris, who never fails to make an appearance. Money to which the committee is entitled is piling up in the bank month by month and plans for the erection of schools in Ballina, Castlebar and Westport are awaiting approval.'

A member of the committee is quoted anonymously as saying, 'We are staying away from the meetings on principle, and not, as has been suggested, to blockade the adoption of the scheme. We will not administer the scheme until the will of the people to appoint whom they wish is recognised ... We know it is hard luck on the teachers to be compelled to go without their salaries, but there you are.'[4]

As 1931 drew to a close the situation seemed as bleak as ever for these teachers. And yet the *Irish Independent* sensed some movement. Under the optimistic headline 'Mayo's Seventeen Unpaid Teachers – Hope for Salaries After Eleven Months', it reported, 'Having waited patiently for almost eleven months the seventeen teachers employed under the Vocational Education Scheme in Mayo hope to be soon paid their salaries again.'[5] The three commercial teachers, one manual instructor, three domestic teachers, four crochet teachers and six whole-time Irish teachers had received no payment due to the committee that authorised their salaries refusing to meet. The *Irish Independent* lamented the plight of these individuals. 'The teachers had to get money from the banks,' wrote the newspaper, 'but whether they would get with their salaries what they had to pay in interest is not yet known.'

The Irish Press reported that Commissioner Bartley had issued an order directing Miss Dunbar Harrison not to give any information to the paper as to the progress or otherwise of the library service of which she had charge. Asked if there was any truth in the rumour that plans were being made for her transfer to Dublin, Miss Dunbar Harrison replied, 'There is no truth whatever in that suggestion which I have heard several times. You can say that I have no intention of leaving Castlebar. I like it very much; the people are very kind and go out of their way to show that they have no animosity to me personally.'[6]

The *Irish Independent* asked the question, 'Will the government do anything about the library crux?' As for the current situation it reported that 'except for the limited support in Castlebar, where persons can get books direct from the library in the county courthouse, the scheme is virtually dead, because the dozens of library committees throughout the county had declined to function.' The *Irish Independent* recognised the complexity of the library stand-off. 'This is a much more difficult problem,' it wrote, 'which, as far as can be seen, the appointment of a whole army of commissioners could not solve, because it is impossible to make the people avail of the library scheme against their wishes.'[7]

Chapter 19

'I like the work and I love the people'

By the start of 1932, with the dispute about to drag on into its second year, there was little sign of a resolution. An impasse had been reached. Miss Dunbar Harrison continued to go about her work in Castlebar while the vast majority of her library centres throughout the county went unused.

P.J. Bartley was still carrying out his duties as Commissioner, but he too was hampered by a lack of co-operation. Many of the council's sub-committees were boycotted, causing severe problems in the education and social welfare sections. The prospect of a general election in the New Year was the one possible change in the political landscape. The Cumann na nGaedheal Party were wary of fighting an election in Mayo with virtually all of their TDs and local representatives opposing their policy on the librarian issue. The cabinet decided to get themselves off the hook by offering Miss Dunbar Harrison an equivalent position in the civil service. This was little more than a flimsy fig-leaf to protect their political vanity. They tried to spin this as a promotion for her, though few people saw it as anything other than a humiliating climb-down on their part.

This solution had been mooted for some time and had long been rumoured in Mayo. It had in fact been suggested to Sir Joseph Glynn in his meetings with members of the Catholic hierarchy as early as spring 1931. The government at the time did not come out and quash this as a possibility.

As with every other aspect of this saga, the government's handling of their climb-down was less than assured. On 2 January *The Irish Times* stated that there was a 'possible post elsewhere'. 'It is reported,' wrote the newspaper, 'that Miss Dunbar Harrison is about to retire from the post of librarian to the Mayo county library at Castlebar … In the conditions which prevailed since her appointment, the usefulness of the library has been greatly circumscribed … Our Castlebar correspondent telegraphing last night, stated that Miss Dunbar Harrison was greatly distressed at the announcement of her resignation, which she declared to be utterly unfounded. Beyond rumour that she was to be transferred, she had heard nothing officially. The commissioner [P.J. Bartley] had not mentioned it to her, and in the circumstances it was unthinkable that she should resign. She added: "I like the work, and I love the people who have shown me every kindness, and I am not likely to resign because some people think I should go elsewhere."'[1]

The Irish Press, had a different slant on the story. Its local correspondent reported a 'sensational development in library dispute', and that 'a curious situation had arisen … Miss Dunbar Harrison, the Mayo librarian, was very indignant when I called on her private residence this morning to interview her about her supposed resignation. "It's a fabrication like the silly lies circulated a few weeks ago by an English newspaper; but I don't mind it, and will not discuss it with you," she vehemently declared … "I have not resigned and have no intention of resigning."'

The *Press* sought a response from the Minister for Local Government. On being asked for a statement Richard Mulcahy said, 'I cannot say whether Miss Harrison's resignation has reached the department or not.'[2] Three days later, undeterred by the denials and confusion, the *Press* confidently stated that a job had been found for Miss Dunbar Harrison in the civil service.

'Is the protracted Mayo librarian controversy about to be ended by the transfer of Miss Dunbar Harrison to a post in the Department of Industry and Commerce?' asked *The Irish Press*. 'The recent announcement in a daily newspaper to the effect that Miss Harrison had resigned was immediately and vigorously denied by

Miss Harrison herself to the Castlebar representative of *The Irish Press*. The secretary of Mayo County Council also stated that he had not received Miss Harrison's resignation. It is now reported that Miss Harrison is about to be transferred to the statistics branch of the Department of Industry and Commerce at, so it is stated, a higher remuneration than the £250 per annum which she is now receiving in Mayo.

'The decision to transfer Miss Harrison was made a month ago, after preliminary local soundings ... a difficulty arose as to the post which would have to be given to her, as in the circumstances she could not be asked to resign ... There is no intention as yet to restore the County Council but such a step may be hinted at in the election campaign.'[3]

On 6 January the *Irish Independent's* banner headline read, 'New Post for County Mayo Librarian'. The same day *The Irish Press* reported that Miss Dunbar Harrison had left Castlebar for Dublin. The prevailing local opinion was that the government, in order to relieve the crisis created by Miss Dunbar Harrison's appointment following the abolition of the County Council, were arranging to transfer her in order to regain the confidence of the Mayo clergy.

The Irish Press also recounted that it was rumoured locally that Miss Dunbar Harrison was to be offered the post of librarian in the Dáil. This yarn seems somewhat mischievous as it is very unlikely that the government would have even contemplated such a move. One can only imagine Letitia Dunbar Harrison working in the same building in which she had been the subject of so much debate the previous June and meeting in the corridors so many of the deputies who had been critical of her, her background and her education. Not only that, one could foresee the Fianna Fáil Party making much political capital of her acknowledged inability to speak Irish.

Confusion reigned for a number of days. It is difficult to believe that the Department of Local Government would decide to move

Miss Dunbar Harrison without first discussing it with her, but initially she seemed genuinely unhappy with the announcement in the newspapers. It would seem that some pressure had to be applied to get her to comply with their suggestion, if suggestion it was, perhaps threatening to forcibly transfer her if she did not agree to go of her own accord. The initial intention may have been to move her to the Department of Industry and Commerce, but the Department of Defence was where she ended up. But as luck would have it, at the same time as the Government was looking around for a position in the Civil Service in Dublin for Miss Dunbar Harrison, the person responsible for the Department of Defence's Military library Mr R.J. Flood, an inveterate memo writer, had been making numerous submissions to his superior officers. He declared that, owing to the shortage of staff and the enormous number of books purchased, he was unable to keep up with his duties. Urgent representations had been made to the Department of Finance in September 1931 'for the provision of badly needed additional staff to cope with essential library work'.

On 8 January *The Irish Press* announced that Miss Dunbar Harrison had returned from Dublin and disclosed that she had accepted a post in the capital. She declined to make a statement but when asked was she satisfied with the change she replied, 'I am delighted with it.' This was, if not quite the end, the beginning of the end. On 16 January *The Irish Press*, which seemed to have very good sources both at a local level in Mayo and at civil service level in Dublin, reported that the Mayo library committee, at a special meeting convened by Commissioner Bartley, had accepted Miss Dunbar Harrison's resignation. She was to hand over her keys to Mr Egan, the County Secretary, on the Tuesday when her resignation took effect, but on the Sunday, 'she became the victim of influenza and was unable to be present'. No date had been given for when she was to take up her duties at the Department of Defence, though it was confidently stated that 'her appointment there will not entail the displacement of any present official of the library.' The *Press* went on to add that 'apart from some works of reference, the library is purely composed of military works.'[4]

Chapter 20

'A rout, not a retreat'

The Irish correspondent of the *Round Table* claimed that the outcome was 'fair to the lady, soothing to the Mayo bigots and good for the government.'[1] This was not a view shared by all. The *Catholic Bulletin* was disapproving of the government's actions. Under the headline 'The Mayo Collapse and its Sequels', it argued, using an extended martial metaphor; 'With his usual ineptitude and even more than his usual clumsiness of procedure, the politico-military bully has evacuated the Mayo front ... So a new post was created: that eminent literary man, Minister Fitzgerald, had to develop a need for a librarian. The pretence of unbending firmness was kept up to the last moment, for with the usual tenacity of the politico-military bully, it was denied and delayed until it was clearly a rout, not a retreat.'[2]

The *Catholic Mind* adopted a slightly different tack. 'It is not putting it too bluntly,' it wrote, 'to state that Miss Dunbar Harrison was ruthlessly sacrificed to the interests of the Cumann na nGaedheal candidates in County Mayo ... it was an act of political corruption, so clumsily performed that no one with any intelligence was fooled by it.'[3] This new-found compassion for Miss Dunbar Harrison was used as a stick with which to beat the government. 'Nobody has apologised yet to Miss Harrison for the indignities to which she has been subjected,' continued the *Catholic Mind*. 'On behalf not only of ourselves but of the Catholics of Mayo whose mind in the matter has been made clear to us by several of the most influential of the clergy of Tuam, we offer her our sympathy ... may Miss Harrison's days be long and happy.'[4] Given all that had gone before one can only wonder at the sincerity of these best wishes.

It is possible to exaggerate the sectarian element to the opposition but, as previously mentioned, a dislike of outsiders was not confined to Mayo. Kathleen White faced similar resistance in Leitrim, if on a lesser scale.

'You have a Clareman's job'

In Clare, Dermot Foley had substantial difficulties when he was appointed county librarian. 'In March 1931, at the tender age of twenty-three, he was recommended for the post of librarian. Initially the council refused to appoint Mr Foley, and proposed to delay his appointment for six months pending the improvement of his knowledge of the Irish language. However, under the threat of legal action from the Department of Local Government, a special meeting was called on 9 July 1931 and it was agreed to appoint Mr Foley.'[5] A Dubliner, he was not exactly welcomed with open arms.[6] As he described it himself, 'An hour or so before the first meeting of the library committee, a small packet was delivered to me by post. It was a tin box marked Oxo, but when I unwrapped the rolled up piece of paper, there were no soup cubes. Instead, out fell two .45 bullets. There was a short message, headed with a skull and cross-bones. "Get out of the county," it said, "you have a Clareman's job."'[7]

The main reason the locals took an instant dislike to Dermot Foley seemed to be that he was taking the job of a good Clareman. This was akin to the argument used against Kathleen White in Leitrim, that by being selected as county librarian, and coming all the way from Laois, she had caused one more poor local to emigrate. This excessive regionalism was essentially a form of xenophobia. The difference in these cases from that of Letitia Dunbar Harrison, was that religion was not an exacerbating factor, fanning the flames. Miss Dunbar Harrison was seen as even more of an outsider, on the grounds of education and class as well as religion. The Irish language, the pretext for her rejection, seemed hardly relevant at all.

Kathleen White survived in Leitrim, as did Dermot Foley, after a fashion, in Clare. He lasted the best part of twenty-three years as county librarian so he was presumably not particularly perturbed by his initial reception. Dermot Foley later moved on to Cork and eventually became director of An Comhairle Leabharlanna, the state's library authority, which was formed in 1947. He had survived in Clare though he did not exactly thrive there, having entered into many a battle with the library committee, the County Council and a specially constituted fifty-strong censorship board.[8]

Letitia Dunbar Harrison on the other hand was never going to last in Mayo. The forces arrayed against her were too strong. While maintaining a strong front publicly, the Cumann na nGaedheal government had tacitly accepted at an early stage of their private meetings with members of the Catholic hierarchy that she would have to be moved. In the transcribed memorandum of the meeting between President Cosgrave and Archbishop Gilmartin on 15 April 1931, it was stated 'that while no promise in writing could be made, and nothing done immediately, if it were possible to do so, the government at a suitable time, would see whether a position elsewhere could be found for Miss Dunbar.'[9] In other words the government was waiting for the opportune moment, when the hubbub had died down, to quietly move her on. With this strategy, as with many of their actions throughout the affair, the government proved unsuccessful. Almost every newspaper pointed out the proximity of a general election as the impetus for Miss Dunbar Harrison's 'promotion' to the Department of Defence in January 1932. In fact the *Catholic Bulletin* insisted on taking things a step further. It accused the government of the Machiavellian policy of backing her while at the same time hoping and indeed encouraging her to resign of her own volition. This would have got them off the hook. It was only when she showed admirable stubbornness that they were forced to act themselves. The outcome of the whole affair could hardly be labelled a victory for central government.

While many people linked the government's movement on the stalemate with the imminent announcement of a general election, it is difficult to gauge the electoral impact of the dispute. The Dáil was dissolved shortly afterwards, on 29 January 1932. The election was held on Tuesday, 16 February. The successful candidates in Mayo received the following first-preference votes.

Mayo North – four seats

P.J. Ruttledge, F.F.	8,690
P. O'Hara, C. na nG.	5,853
M. Davis, C. na nG.	5,809
M. Clery, F.F.	5,443

Mayo South – five seats

J. Fitzgerald-Kenney, C. na nG.	7,041
R. Walsh, F.F.	6,945
M. Kilroy, F.F.	5,589
E. Moane, F.F.	4,711
M. Nally, C. na nG.	3,414

Fianna Fáil gained one seat in Mayo but at the expense, not of Cumann na nGaedheal, but of the Labour Party, whose leader T.J. O'Connell lost his seat in Mayo South. Thomas O'Connell, who was also general secretary of the Irish National Teachers' Organisation, had opposed the appointment of Letitia Dunbar Harrison on the basis that his party had not agreed with the setting up of the Local Appointments Commission in the first place. He had also questioned the dissolution of Mayo County Council. There is no record of him speaking out against the sectarian element of the antagonism towards Miss Dunbar Harrison as might have been expected of the leader of the Labour Party.

Prior to the assassination of Kevin O'Higgins, the Labour Party had led the parliamentary resistance to the incumbent government, but once Fianna Fáil had changed their abstentionist policy and taken their seats, the Labour Party found itself vying with the numerically superior Fianna Fáil to make an impact. *The Watchword* of Labour, the party's weekly newspaper had, on the other hand, been broadly supportive of the government's actions. It is more likely that Thomas O'Connell's silence on the sectarian component of the disagreement was for purely local reasons, and that realising what a contentious issue it was, he had tried not to antagonise anybody. Overall, Labour's nationwide performance in the election was atrocious. Of the party's thirty-three candidates, just under half lost their deposits.[10]

Moreover, it cannot be said that Mr O'Connell lost his seat in Mayo due to his actions or his inaction with regard to the Miss Dunbar Harrison affair. In fact it is difficult to see what effect, if any, the affair had on the voting patterns in Mayo. The librarian issue cannot be said to have had a drastic effect on the Cumann na nGaedheal Party vote but as most of their public representatives had taken an anti-government stance on the controversy that hardly proves anything one way or the other. Mr Fitzgerald-Kenney, the outgoing Minister for Justice and the only Mayo TD to vote with the government in the Dáil debate on 17 June 1931, actually topped the poll in Mayo South.

Nationwide Fianna Fáil won seventy-two seats compared to fifty-six seats for Cumann na nGaedheal. The Labour Party lost six seats. On 9 March Eamon de Valera was elected President of the Executive Council by eighty-one votes to sixty-eight. Mayo TD P.J. Ruttledge was appointed Minister for Agriculture in the new administration.

It was a number of years before the new government eventually restored Mayo County Council. Commissioner P.J. Bartley maintained a good working relationship with Fianna Fáil, and at a later date he was appointed commissioner to Westmeath and to Laois. In 1942, following the Local Government (County Management) Act of 1940, he became one of the first newly created county managers for Laois where he had previously acted as Commissioner. One could argue that county managers were given many of the executive functions that commissioners had exercised in the past, so P.J. Bartley was well suited to his new role.

One other civil servant was not quite so fortunate. Fianna Fáil's antipathy to E.P. McCarron had not abated. In 1935 he was dismissed after falling out with his new minister, Seán T. O'Kelly. He was one of the few secretaries of departments in the history of the state to be clearly forced out of office due to a dispute with his minister. The immediate cause of his removal was that he was accused of exceeding his authority in sanctioning an appointment to a medical post in Grangegorman and Portrane mental hospitals.[11] The government could at least take some satisfaction in their stout defence of the Local Appointments Commission. If they had allowed Mayo County Council to overrule its recommendation it is doubtful that the LAC could have survived. The LAC together with the Civil Service Commission are generally regarded as examples of the successes of the Cumann na nGaedheal government's decade in office. The merit-based central recruitment agency is still in existence today. In 2004 the civil service and Local Appointments Commission were merged into one body, becoming the Public Appointments Service. As regards recruitment, librarians are still required to have a working knowledge of Irish.

Mayo County Council was not restored until May 1932, following a prolonged eight-hour meeting. Canon McHugh, who was a supporter of Commissioner Bartley, was removed from all committees. Rev. Jackson and Dr McBride were also voted off the library committee.[12] The post of county librarian in Mayo was eventually filled in October 1932 by Kathleen Ronaldson, who had been an assistant librarian in Galway. Incidentally, she was a Catholic.

Chapter 21

'Inner emigration'

The actions of Mayo County Council did not go unnoticed in the North of Ireland. St John Ervine, in his biography of Lord Craigavon published in 1949, gave a detailed account of the dispute. 'It is dangerous,' he concluded, 'apparently, to the faith and morals of an Irish Roman Catholic to receive across a library counter a copy of *David Copperfield*; if, that is to say, *David Copperfield*, which was written by a Protestant, and one, moreover, who was antipathetic to Roman Catholicism, would be permitted to lie on the bookshelves of Ballinrobe and Ballina.'[1]

Seán O Faoláin, in his biography of Eamon de Valera, published in 1939, declared that while the pious aspirations of the Constitution might guarantee religious tolerance, there was as little chance of Protestants in the South getting the same share of public appointments as Catholics in the North. He then referred to 'the furore raised when a Protestant girl was appointed librarian in Mayo...' He concluded that, 'Neither North nor South need pretend that the other is alone in this kind of penalisation on account of religion and private opinion. Religion in the South is just as solidly organised as in the North, and is no less narrowminded.'

Discrimination in the North was much remarked upon. Reactions differed. Anything that they can do, we can do too, was one response. No matter what was done down South it was worse up there, was another.

In later years the Mayo librarian affair was seen as a telling moment in church-state relations in the formative years of the Free State. Michael D. Higgins was particularly critical of Fianna Fáil's stance. 'De Valera,' he said, 'had provided the good people of

Irishtown with an exercise in casuistry that must have left the three-card-trick man of Ballinrobe Races without a shred of credibility. If the librarianship was an "educative" post, he could understand Catholics requiring to be recommended books by a Catholic librarian and so on. If Miss Letitia was suddenly dumb she would no doubt have satisfied.'[2]

De Valera's standpoint on the Mayo librarian issue has been criticised. Garret Fitzgerald mentioned the affair in a critical analysis of Eamon de Valera's constitutional politics, which he saw as sectarian. Historian John A. Murphy, in a senate debate in 1981, referred to the outcome of the affair, stating that Letitia Dunbar Harrison was transferred 'to an army barracks where it is presumed the denizens were too corrupt to be corrupted by a Protestant librarian.'[3] Diarmuid Ferriter in his broadly favourable recent biography of de Valera describes his attitude to the issue as 'regrettable'. T.P. O'Neill, an earlier biographer, also defended his subject against any claim of sectarianism. 'De Valera's statement,' he wrote, 'was certainly not as considered as his later speeches were but he is not alone in that.' Mr O'Neill added, 'The whole affair was ineptly handled by the government of the day.'[4] Undoubtedly, the Cumann na nGaedheal government's handling of the crisis was less than assured. Always one step behind, they appeared to react to circumstances rather than to take control of the situation.

The segregation of the Protestant minority in the new state was much remarked upon. Even Trinity College had suffered a crisis of confidence in the aftermath of Independence. As one history of the university puts it, the period was one of 'adjustment and survival', where 'the most unhealthy aspect of the college's situation was its growing isolation from the main currents of national life.'[5]

Hubert Butler was a Protestant who had himself worked with Sir Horace Plunkett as a librarian in Ireland in the 1920s. In 1955 he went forward as a candidate for election to Kilkenny

County Council. He was not successful. In an election address at the time, he spoke about the cultural and political isolation of the Protestant minority. He was particularly critical of the Protestant community for not getting more involved in Irish society in the twenty-six counties in the immediate aftermath of Independence. 'As an Irish county librarian,' he declared, 'I saw many years ago how it was usually through their own inertia that Irish Protestants lost cultural influence in the provinces.'[6] Referring directly to the Mayo librarian affair, he commented, 'The government supported the Protestant candidate, but their stand received only lukewarm support from the Protestant community and ultimately the government capitulated.'[7]

Neal Ascherson, in his introduction to a collection of Hubert Butler's writings, refers to this isolation as a form of 'inner emigration'.

'Mayo was right'

It is little wonder that the minority community were nervous. In March 1932, there was an attempt by the *Catholic Mind* to broaden the scope of the Mayo affair by stirring up a similar quarrel in Cork. The *Catholic Mind* published an anonymous letter in which the writer complained that it was impossible to get a Catholic Bible in Cork city library, whose librarian, a certain Mr Wilkinson, was a Protestant. According to the periodical, 'This case proves that it is the librarian who counts. No matter how well disposed the non-Catholic librarian may be, he cannot possibly be expected to get inside the Catholic mind. Mayo was right.'[8] Given the lack of local support, this controversy fizzled out, but public servants like Mr Wilkinson can hardly have felt secure given what had happened in Mayo. It would be a mistake, however, to assume that the most vehement and vocal opposition to Letitia Dunbar Harrison's appointment was representative of general opinion in the country.

'Violence of language ... extreme virulence ... scorn and obloquy'

In 1936 Fr Stephen Brown published a commentary that was severely critical of the *Catholic Bulletin*. 'The tone of editorials and articles,' he wrote, 'was marked by violence of language. The Cosgrave government was assailed in every issue with extreme virulence. And both Catholics and Protestants who did not meet with the editor's approval were held up to scorn and obloquy.' In reply to this outright attack, Fr Brown's fellow Jesuit, Fr Timothy Corcoran, seemed quite happy to accept the charge of extremism. 'For Catholics who deliberately place themselves in contact with plague-bearing insects,' Fr Corcoran said, 'a drastic disinfection process is quite in order ... persons whose ebullient brains are poorly underpinned by wobbly knees.'[9]

Some personal joy had come of Letitia Dunbar Harrison's time in Mayo. She had met Rev. Robert C. Crawford, a Methodist minister originally from Belfast who was based in Castlebar at the time. They were married in St Philip's Church, Milltown, County Dublin, at the end of June 1932, by which stage Rev. Crawford had finished his five-year stint in Mayo and had transferred to Dundalk. Letitia Dunbar Harrison worked in the Military Library based in Parkgate Street for just a short period. Her colleague Mr Flood has left a description of the working conditions there:

> The present library premises, though suitable as a housing room for books does not answer the purpose for clerical duties. The room is long and very draughty. There are six ventilators and all seem to be open and out of order. The fire is continually smoking and distributing soot and fine ashes around the place. The windows are all loose and create an abominable noise even in the slightest breeze. On a very windy day it is impossible to concentrate on work with the din created.[10]

Letitia Dunbar Harrison's duty as librarian consisted mainly in organising the purchase of books such as *Elements of Imperial*

Defence, The Battle of Dora and The Intelligence Service – Canadian Corps. Their spending fund for the year April 1931–March 1932 was £600.

On her marriage, Letitia resigned and Mr R.J. Flood returned to writing letters of supplication to his superiors. On 17 July 1932 he wrote, 'the resignation of Miss Letitia Harrison in June last has had the effect of imposing extra duties on me and at the moment I find myself again in the unhappy position of combining two jobs in the working time of one.'

In his career as a Methodist minister, Rev. Crawford served in a number of towns during the 1930s and 1940s. He and Letitia travelled several of the southern circuits. They lived for some time in Dundalk, followed by Adare and Roscrea. In later years the couple settled in Whitehead in Northern Ireland, a coastal town near Carrickfergus not far from Belfast, where Rev. Crawford exercised his ministry. Letitia suffered the premature loss of her husband after just twenty years of marriage when Rev. Crawford died in 1952. The death notice in *The Irish Times* described him as a 'dearly loved husband'.[11]

By this stage, Letitia Dunbar Harrison was known as Aileen Crawford, and was perhaps happy to spend her days in quiet obscurity, living out her life away from the glare of controversy and public scrutiny that had plagued her in the Free State. She did, however, have at least one other brush with authority in her lifetime. After her husband's death Aileen Crawford 'developed the conviction that she should continue his work.'[12] She successfully completed her local preachers' examinations and became an accredited local preacher. Much to the consternation of the Methodist church in Ireland, she then presented herself as a candidate for the ministry; she was the first Irish woman to do so. The board of examiners 'could find nothing in the rules as then formulated to say that all candidates must be men.' However, to the undoubted relief of the board, Mrs Crawford failed one of the written examinations, the one on knowledge of the scriptures. Nevertheless, as the first woman to apply for the ministry she was the catalyst that led to the Methodist church in Ireland in 1954 considering the matter of women ministers. A report was presented at conference in 1955. The Theological Committee found that 'there is no obstacle in Holy Scripture, in the tradition of the church, or in the nature of woman to prevent the ordination of women to a separated ministry in the church.'

Turning to the practicalities of the matter, the committee discussed the physical strain involved in many of the country circuits, the attitude of individual circuits to the appointment of a woman as their minister and the effect on circuit work of the possible claims of motherhood and domestic responsibilities. They then indicated the first essentials that must be satisfied before a woman could be admitted, and these were three:

1. The legal alteration of the Constitution.
2. The elucidation of the problem, both legal and practical, of the occupancy of the manses by men not subject to Methodist discipline.
3. The re-adjustment of the regulations governing the administration of the supernumerary, children's and annuitant funds.

Given that list of essentials, it will come as no surprise that the membership of the Theological and Sectional Committees was entirely male. The report concluded that, 'In view of the absence of any clearly defined or generally expressed desire on the part of our people for the admission of women into the full ministry of our church, no legislative action be taken at this juncture.'[13]

Essentially it was felt that while there was no doctrinal reason why women could not be ministers, there were a number of practical considerations, the most telling of which was that it was felt that none of the circuits at that time were likely to employ a woman. Though nothing came of the debate at that time, it was to remain a live issue in the Methodist church for the following decades. The first woman Methodist minister was not ordained until the mid-1970s.

Perhaps Aileen Crawford had been naïve in accepting the post in Mayo in the first place, given the level of opposition she was bound to encounter. But then jobs were not that easy to come by for educated young women in Ireland in the 1930s. And she did not have the safeguard of any employment legislation to protect her from discrimination as she undoubtedly would if the same situation occurred today.

Aileen Crawford redirected her energies to other areas. She showed a strong interest in the temperance movement and was a school lecturer for the temperance board. She also became heavily involved in the Methodist Women's Association and was the all-Ireland secretary from 1945 to 1959 and subsequently all-Ireland president from 1959 to 1962. Her interest in the temperance movement led to a visit to Delhi in 1962 as a delegate to a White Ribbon Conference, from where she went to visit the missionaries Dorothy Robb in South India and George Good in Sri Lanka. She was also involved with Meals on Wheels and a friendship club for pensioners at University Road Methodist church.[14]

Following in the footsteps of her husband, Aileen Crawford was a regular contributor to the Methodist paper, the *Irish Christian Advocate*, first writing under the pseudonym 'Miss Silver Birch, BA'. When she married, she became just 'Silver Birch, BA'. And when she acquired an MA from Trinity College in her later years (i.e. she purchased it), the byline on her articles was changed from 'Silver Birch, BA' to 'Silver Birch, MA'.

Given Aileen Crawford's treatment at the hands of the government, Mayo County Council and the people of Mayo, it is hardly surprising that she did not pursue a career in librarianship. She died in Belfast in October 1994 at the fine old age of eighty-eight.

Notes

Introduction
1   *Roscommon Herald*, 3 January 1931, p.4.
2   Ibid.
3   Ibid.
4   *Irish Independent*, 29 December 1930, p.5.
5   *Roscommon Herald*, 3 January 1931, p.4.
6   *Irish Independent*, 28 December 1930, p.5.
7   *Roscommon Herald*, 3 January 1931, p.4.

Chapter 1
1   *The Connaught Telegraph*, 1 November 1930, p.4.
2   Ibid., 29 November 1930, p.3.
3   Ibid., 6 December 1930, p.8.
4   Ibid.
5   Ibid.
6   Ibid.
7   Ibid.
8   *Mayo News*, 6 December 1930, p.5.
9   *The Connaught Telegraph*, 6 December 1930, p.8.
10 Ibid.
11 *Mayo News*, 6 December 1930, p.5.
12 Ibid.
13 *The Connaught Telegraph*, 6 December 1930, p.8.

Chapter 2
1   *The Irish Times*, 3 December 1930, p.6.
2   *The Church of Ireland Gazette*, 5 December 1930, p.684.
3   *The Irish Times*, 6 December 1930, p.6.
4   *Irish Independent,* 11 December 1930, p.10.
5   Ibid., p.12.
6   *Irish Independent*, 13 December 1930, p.12.
7   Ibid., 18 December 1930, p.9.
8   Ibid., 13 December 1930, p.12.
9   *Mayo News*, 27 December 1930, p.6.
10 *The Watchword*, 3 January 1931, p.1.
11 *The Connaught Telegraph*, 6 December 1930, p.4.
12 Ibid., 13 December 1930, p.6.

Chapter 3

1   *The Connaught Telegraph*, 13 December 1930, p.6.
2   Desmond Roche, *Local Government in Ireland*, p.124.
3   *Mayo News*, 13 December 1930, p.7.
4   *The Connaught Telegraph*, 13 December 1930, p.6.
5   Ibid.
6   Ibid.
7   *Irish Independent*, 9 December 1930, p.9.
8   Ibid., 10 December 1930, p.5.
9   *The Irish Times*, 19 December 1930, p.5.
10 Ibid.
11 *Irish Independent*, 10 December 1930, p.9.
12 Ibid.
13 Dáil Debate, 11 December 1930.
14 Ibid.
15 *Irish Independent*, 9 December 1930, p.9.
16 *The Nation*, 13 December 1930, p.1.
17 *Irish Independent*, 19 December 1930, p.10.
18 *The Watchword*, 20 December 1930, p.1.
19 *The Connaught Telegraph*, 13 December 1930, p.4.
20 *Catholic Mind*, vol. iii, no. 2, February 1932, p.31.
21 *Western People*, 13 December 1930, p.7.
22 Ibid.
23 Ibid.

Chapter 4

1   *Western People*, 20 December 1930, p.3.
2   *The Connaught Telegraph*, 20 December 1930, p.5.
3   *Western People*, 20 December 1930, p.3.
4   *The Connaught Telegraph*, 20 December 1930, p.5.
5   *Mayo News*, 20 December 1930, p.5.
6   Ibid.
7   Dáil Debates, 1 March 1922.
8   Mary E. Daly, *The Buffer State: The Historical Roots of the Department of the Environment* p. 99.
9   *Mayo News*, 20 December 1930, p.5.
10 *Leitrim Observer*, 20 December 1930, p.1.
11 *Irish Independent*, 22 December 1930, p.6.
12 Ibid., 24 December 1930, p.8.
13 *The Connaught Telegraph*, 27 December 1930, p.5.
14 *Leitrim Observer*, 27 December 1930, p.4.

Chapter 5

1 Desmond Roche, *Local Government in Ireland*, p. 53.
2 Brendan Grimes, *Irish Carnegie Libraries*, p.54.
3 'The Limerick New Public Library and Museum', *An Leabharlann*, March 1907, vol. ii, no. 2, p.141.
4 Ibid., pp. 123-143.
5 Dáil Debates, 8 June 1928.
6 Ibid., 19 May 1926.
7 Ibid.
8 Ibid.
9 Ibid., 20 May 1926.
10 Ibid.
11 Ibid.
12 Ibid., 22 June 1926.
13 Ibid., 1 June 1928.
14 Ibid., 6 June 1928.
15 Ibid., 8 June 1928.
16 Ibid., 13 June 1928.
17 Ibid., 22 June 1928.
18 *The Connaught Telegraph*, 7 February 1931, p.6.

Chapter 6

1 *Western People*, 3 January 1931, p.7.
2 *Roscommon Herald*, 3 January 1931, p.4.
3 Ibid.
4 *The Connaught Telegraph*, 3 January 1931, p.5.
5 *Roscommon Herald*, 3 January 1931, p.4.
6 *Western People*, 3 January 1931, p.7.
7 Ibid.
8 *Roscommon Herald*, 3 January 1931, p.4.
9 *Western People*, 3 January 1931, p.7.
10 Ibid.
11 *Roscommon Herald*, 3 January 1931, p.4.
12 *Western People*, 3 January 1931, p.7.
13 Ibid.
14 *Roscommon Herald*, 3 January 1931, p.4.
15 *Western People*, 3 January 1931, p.7.
16 Ibid. This is a line from Walter Scott's *The Lady in the Lake*.
17 Ibid. This lengthy quotation is from A.M. Sullivan's verses on Brian Boru's address to his army before the Battle of Clontarf.
18 *Western People*, 3 January 1931, p.9.

19   *Roscommon Herald*, 3 January 1931, p.4.

20   *Western People*, 3 January 1931, p.9.

21   *Roscommon Herald*, 3 January 1931, p.4.

22   *Western People*, 3 January 1931, p.9.

23   Ibid.

24   *Roscommon Herald*, 3 January 1931, p.4.

25   Ibid.

26   *Western People*, 3 January 1931, p.9.

27   Ibid.

28   Ibid.

29   *Roscommon Herald*, 3 January 1931, p.4.

30   Ibid.

31   Ibid.

32   *Western People*, 3 January 1931, p.9.

33   *Roscommon Herald*, 3 January 1931, p.4.

34   Ibid.

Chapter 7

1   *Irish Independent*, 31 December 1930, p.7.

2   *Cork Examiner*, 29 December 1930, p.7.

3   Desmond Roche, op. cit., p. 53.

4   Ibid.

5   *Leitrim Observer*, 10 January 1931, p.2.

6   *The Connaught Telegraph*, 10 January 1931, p.6.

7   *Mayo News*, 3 January 1931, p.7.

8   Ibid.

9   Michael Kennedy, *Division and Consensus*, p.25.

10   *Catholic Bulletin*, vol. 21, no. 2, 1931. Quoted by Dermot Keogh, *Twentieth-Century Ireland*, p.57.

11   *Irish Independent*, 5 January 1931, p.8.

12   *Methodist Newsletter*, December 1994, p.4.

13   *Western People*, 3 January 1931, p.3.

Chapter 8

1   Lennox Robinson, 'The Irish Work of the Carnegie Trust', *Proceedings of the Irish Library Conference*, 1923, p.27.

2   Quoted in Abigail A. Van Slyck, *Free to All: Carnegie Libraries and American Culture 1890-1920*.

3   Lennox Robinson, *Curtain Up*, p.84.

4   Ibid., p.83.

5   Lennox Robinson, 'The Irish Work of the Carnegie Trust', *Proceedings*

of the Irish Library Conference, 1923, p.29.

6 Roísín Walsh, 'Libraries' in *Saorstát Éireann Official Handbook* (1932), p.210.

7 Lt Col J.M. Mitchell, 'Public Libraries', *Proceedings of the Irish Library Conference* 1923, pp.16-17.

8 Christina Keogh, *The County Library System in Ireland 1929*, p.9.

9 Christina Keogh, *Report on Public Library Provision in the Irish Free State, 1935*, p.11.

10 Ibid., p.14.

11 Brigid Redmond, 'In the Middle of the County Mayo', *Capuchin Annual* 1932, pp. 166-180.

12 *The Meath Chronicle*, 21 February 1931, p.1.

13 Terence Brown, *A Social and Cultural History 1922-2001*, pp.74-75.

14 Lennox Robinson, *Curtain Up*, p.135.

15 Roísín Walsh, 'Libraries' in *Saorstát Éireann Official Handbook* (1932), p.210.

16 Dermot Foley, 'A Minstrel Boy with a Satchel of Books', *Irish University Review*, autumn 1974, p.209.

17 Seán O Súilleabháin, *Leabharlann Chontae Liatroma 75 Blian ar an Saol*, p.17.

18 Roísín Walsh, 'County Dublin Library Scheme', *An Leabharlann*, vol. 1, no. 1, June 1930, pp.20-21.

19 Christina Keogh, *The County Library System in Ireland 1929*, p.10.

20 *The Anglo-Celt*, 10 January 1931, p.1.

21 Seán Ó Súilleabháin, op. cit., p.2.

22 Dermot Foley, 'A Minstrel Boy with a Satchel of Books', op. cit., p.208.

23 Seán Ó Súilleabháin, op. cit., p.6.

24 Brigid Redmond, op. cit., p.166.

25 Ibid., p.167.

26 Ibid.

27 Helen Roe, 'Laoighis County Libraries', *An Leabharlann*, vol. 3, no. 1, April 1933, p.8.

28 Brigid Redmond, op. cit., p.167.

29 Ibid.

30 Christina Keogh, *Report on Public Library Provision in the Irish Free State, 1935*, p.14.

31 Rev. J. Butler, 'The Committee-man Plays his Part', *An Leabharlann*, vol. 7, no. 1, December 1939, p.12.

32 Ibid.

33 Brigid Redmond, op. cit., p.170.

34 Dermot Foley, op. cit., p.209.

35 Brigid Redmond, op. cit., p.171.

36 Ibid., p.175.

37 Ibid., p.177.

38 Ibid., p.178.

39 Ibid., p.179.

40 Ibid.

41 Helen Roe, op. cit., p.8.

42 Brigid Redmond, op. cit., p.167.

43 Christina Keogh, *Report on Public Library Provision in the Irish Free State, 1935,* p.15.

44 Ibid., p.18.

45 *Mayo News*, 17 January 1931, p.8.

Chapter 9

1   *Irish Independent*, 30 December 1930, p.9.

2   *Western People*, 3 January 1931, p.3.

3   NAI D/Taioseach S2547A.

4   *Irish Independent*, 12 January 1931, p.8.

5   *The Watchword*, 3 January 1931, p.1.

6   Ibid.

7   *The Nation*, 5 January 1931, p.1.

8   *Western People*, 21 February 1931, p.3.

9   Michael Davitt, *Leaves from a Prison Diary*, pp.182-184.

10 *The Connaught Telegraph*, 10 January 1931, p.1.

11 *Ibid.*

12 *An Reult,* January 1931, p.1.

13 NAI D/Taioseach S2547A.

14 *Mayo News*, 17 January 1931, p.8.

15 *The Irish Times*, 16 January 1931, p.5.

16 *Irish Independent*, 27 January 1931, p.8.

17 Ibid., 26 February 1931, p.7.

Chapter 10

1   *Evening Herald*, 5 January 1931, p.8.

2   *The Anglo-Celt*, 10 January 1931, p.1.

3   Local authorities at the time were funded by rates. In the estimates for the forthcoming year a certain proportion would be put aside for each item of expenditure.

4   *The Anglo-Celt*, 10 January 1931, p.1.

5   *Sligo Champion*, 10 January 1931, p.3.

6   *The Anglo-Celt*, 10 January 1931, p.5.

7　*The Connaught Telegraph*, 10 January 1931, p. 7. *The Sorrows of Satan* is a novel by Marie Corelli.
8　*Sligo Champion*, 10 January 1931, p.3.
9　*The Anglo-Celt*, 10 January 1931, p.5.
10　Ibid., 10 January 1931, p.5.
11　*Evening Herald*, 5 January 1931, p.8.
12　*Irish Independent*, 6 January 1931, p.9.
13　*Sligo Champion*, 10 January 1931, p.3.
14　Ibid.
15　Ibid.
16　*The Connaught Telegraph*, 10 January 1931, p.7.
17　*Leitrim Observer*, 24 January 1931, p.1.
18　*Irish Independent*, 23 January 1931, p.7.
19　*The Anglo-Celt*, 31 January 1931, p.10.
20　*Irish Independent*, 26 January 1931, p.10.
21　*The Anglo-Celt*, 2 November 1929, p.10.
22　*Leitrim Observer*, 31 January 1931, p.1.
23　Ibid.

Chapter 11

1　*Catholic Bulletin*, March 1931, vol. xxi, no. 3, p.211.
2　*Western People*, 5 January 1931, p.1.
3　*Irish Independent*, 7 January 1931, p.7.
4　*Connaught Tribune*, 3 January 1931, p.5.
5　*Mayo News*, 24 January 1931, p.7.
6　*Roscommon Herald*, 14 February 1931, p.3.
7　*The Connaught Telegraph*, 10 January 1931, p.7.
8　*Mayo News*, 17 January 1931, p.8.
9　*Western People*, 17 January 1931, p.12.
10　*Irish Independent*, 24 January 1931, p.4.
11　*Western People*, 24 January 1931, p.6.
12　*Irish Independent*, 26 February 1931, p.4.
13　*Catholic Bulletin*, vol. xxi, no. 4, 1931, p.323.
14　Paul Blanshard, *The Irish and Catholic Power,* pp.100-112.
15　Charles Arthur Boycott, *Boycott*.
16　In 1957 a dispute arose in Fethard-on-Sea, a small village in County Wexford over two children from a mixed marriage. A Catholic farmer had married a Protestant woman. The couple later disagreed over whether their children should be raised as Catholics or Protestants. This led to the boycotting of the local minority Protestant population by their Catholic neighbours.

17 *Western People*, 24 January 1931, p.3.

Chapter 12

1   *Catholic Bulletin*, January 1931, vol. xxi, no. 1, pp.1-2.
2   Ibid., February 1931, vol. xxi, no. 1, pp.102-103.
3   *Catholic Standard*, 30 December 1930, p.10.
4   *The Nation*, 30 December 1930, p.1.
5   *Catholic Mind*, January 1931, pp.1-4.
6   Ibid., February 1931, p.28.
7   NAI D/Taioseach S2547B.
8   Ibid.
9   Ibid.
10 Ibid.
11 Ibid.
12 Anthony J. Jordan, *W. T. Cosgrave 1880-1965*, p.130.
13 NAI D/Taioseach S2547A.
14 James Meenan, *George O'Brien*, p.134.
15 Brian P. Murphy, *The Catholic Bulletin and Republican Ireland*, pp.274-282.
16 Bryan Fanning, *The Quest for Modern Ireland: The Battle of Ideas 1912-1986*, p.67.
17 Brian P. Murphy, op. cit., pp.274-282.
18 NAI D/Taioseach S2547B.
19 Margaret O'Callaghan, 'Language, Nationality and Cultural Identity in the Irish Free State, 1922-1927', p.275.
20 NAI D/Taioseach S2547B.
21 Ibid.
22 Ibid.

Chapter 13

1   *Catholic Bulletin*, January 1931, vol. xxi, no. 1, pp.6-7.
2   Brigid Redmond, op. cit., p.173.
3   Ibid.
4   Henry Dixon, 'The Corporation and the Bible in Irish', *An Leabhar-lann*, March 1907, vol. ii, no. 2, pp.188-189.
5   R.J. Bennett, *Seán na Sagart, the priest hunter*, pp.5-6.
6   R.J. Bennett, postscript p.21. The author notes that these placenames were related to him by an old storyteller from Tourmakeady, which may account for the phonetic spellings of the townlands.
7   Matthew Archdeacon, *Shawn na Soggart*, p.415.
8   Ibid.

9   *Enniscorthy Echo*, 3 January 1931, p.6.

10 *The Church of Ireland Gazette*, 19 December 1930, p.727.

11 Ibid., 24 December 1930, p.736.

12 Miriam Moffitt, *The Church of Ireland Community of Killala & Achonry, 1870-1940*, p.10.

Chapter 14

1   *Irish Independent*, 8 December 1930, p.11.

2   *Catholic Bulletin*, vol. xiv, no. 4, April 1924, p.269.

3   *Cork Examiner*, 12 January 1931, p.7.

4   *The Irish Times*, 9 April 1931, p.8.

5   Ibid.

6   Ibid.

7   J.J. Lee, *Ireland 1912-1985: Politics and Society*, p.164.

8   *An Phoblacht*, Xmas Number 1930, p.4.

9   *An Phoblacht*, 10 January 1931, p.1.

10 J.J. Lee, op. cit., p.164.

11 *The Connaught Telegraph*, 3 January 1931, p.8.

12 Stephen Brown, *A Guide to Books on Ireland*, p.x.

13 Stephen Brown, *Ireland in Fiction*, p.xii.

14 Mary E. Daly, *The Buffer State*, p.167.

15 *Catholic Bulletin*, vol. xxi, no. 4, April 1931, p.322.

16 F.S.L. Lyons, *Culture and Anarchy in Ireland*, p.82.

Chapter 15

1   NAI D/Taioseach S2547B.

2   Ibid.

3   *Irish Independent*, 9 December 1930, p.9.

4   NAI D/Taioseach S2547B.

5   Ibid.

6   *Irish Independent*, 9 December 1930, p.9.

7   Sheamus Smyth, *Off Screen: A Memoir*, p.205.

8   Kevin Rockett, *Irish Film Censorship*, p.63.

9   *The Irish Times*, 4 April 1925, p.6.

10 *Catholic Mind*, vol. 1, no. 10, November 1930, p.273.

11 Terence Brown, *Ireland: A Social and Cultural History 1922-2001*, p.189.

12 *Irish Independent*, 12 March 1943, p.3.

13 Eunan O'Halpin, *Defending Ireland*, p.187.

14 Richard Hayes Papers, National Library, 22984 (6).

15 Martin Hartline & M.M. Kaulbach, *CIA Study: Michael Collins and Bloody*

Sunday, https://www.cia.gov/library/center-for-the-study-of-intelligence/kent-csi/docs/v13i1a06p_0004.htm.

16 David Neligan, *The Spy in the Castle*, pp.78-79.

17 Tim Pat Coogan, *Michael Collins*, pp.76-78.

18 David Neligan, op. cit., p.79.

19 Martin Maguire, *Servants to the Public: A History of the Local Government and Public Servants Union 1901-1990*, p.276.

20 *An Leabharlann*, vol. 11, no. 1, March 1953, p.31.

21 Dermot Foley, *An Leabharlann*, vol. 21, no. 3, September 1963, p.77.

22 Ibid.

23 Ibid.

24 Quoted by Paul Blanshard, *The Irish and Catholic Power*, pp.110-112.

25 Stephen Brown, *Libraries and Literature From a Catholic Standpoint*, p.92.

26 Ibid.

27 LAI Minutes Book, 1928-1931, LAI Archives, Box 3.

28 Ibid.

29 *An Leabharlann*, vol. 1, no. 1, June 1930, pp.16-19.

30 *An Leabharlann*, vol. 1, no. 4, March-May 1931, p.97.

31 *Irish Independent*, 24 January 1931, p.4.

32 Ibid.

33 LAI, *Report of the Executive Board Oct. 1928–Apr. 1929*, p.5.

Chapter 16

1 *Catholic Bulletin*, January 1931, vol. xxi, no. 1., p.16.

2 Quoted by Margaret O'Callagahan, 'Language, Nationality and Cultural Identity in the Irish Free State, 1922-1927', *Irish Historical Studies*, vol. 24, no. 94, November 1984, p.275.

3 Dáil Debates, 1 June 1928.

4 Mary E. Daly, op. cit., p.133.

5 *Catholic Bulletin*, vol. xxi, no. 1, January 1931, p.18.

6 LAI Minutes Book, 1928-1931, LAI Archives, Box 3.

7 NAI D/Taioseach S2547A.

8 Newspaper clipping, undated, LAI Archives Box 1.

9 Rosemary Cullen Owens, *A Social History of Women in Ireland 1870-1970*, p.265.

10 Seán Ó Súilleabháin, op. cit., p.16.

11 NAI D/Taioseach S2547A.

12 Ibid.

13 *Irish Independent*, 17 June 1931, p.5.

14 *The Irish Times*, 17 June 1931, p.7.

Chapter 17

1   Dáil Debates, 17 June 1931.
2   Ibid.
3   Ibid.
4   Ibid.
5   Ibid.
6   Ibid.
7   Ibid.
8   Ibid.
9   Ibid.
10 Ibid.
11 Ibid.
12 Ibid.
13 *The Irish Times*, 18 June 1931, p.8.
14 Ibid.
15 Quoted in *The Irish Times*, 22 June 1931, p.7.
16 *Catholic Bulletin*, vol. xxi, no. 7, July 1931, p.310.

Chapter 18

1   UCD Archives, Mulcahy Collection, P7b.
2   Ibid.
3   *Connacht Sentinel*, 15 September 1931, p.4.
4   *Irish Press*, 30 September 1931, p.1.
5   *Irish Independent*, 14 November 1931, p.5.
6   *Irish Press*, 30 September 1931, p.1.
7   *Irish Independent*, 14 November 1931, p.5.

Chapter 19

1   *The Irish Times*, 2 January 1932, p.7.
2   *Irish Press*, 2 January 1932, p.1.
3   Ibid., 5 January 1932, p.1.
4   Ibid., 16 January 1932, p.4.

Chapter 20

1   Quoted by Dermot Keogh, *Twentieth-Century Ireland*, p.58.
2   *Catholic Bulletin*, vol. xxii, no. 2, February 1932, p.60.
3   *Catholic Mind*, vol. iii, no. 2, February 1932, p.31.
4   Ibid.
5   www.clarelibrary.ie/eolas/library/history/colibser.htm.
6   *Clare Champion*, 25 September 1998, p.13.
7   Dermot Foley, op. cit., p.208.
8   Ibid.

9   NAI D/Taioseach S2547B.

10   Niamh Puirseil, *The Irish Labour Party 1922-73,* p. 37.

11   Mary E. Daly, op. cit., p.163.

12   *Connacht Sentinel,* 3 May 1932, p.4.

Chapter 21

1   St John Ervine, *Craigavon Ulsterman,* p.41.

2   *City Tribune,* 21 August 1987, p.10.

3   Seanad Eireann Debates, 9 October 1981.

4   *The Irish Times,* 1 March 1982, p.10.

5   J.V. Luce, *Trinity College Dublin: The First 400 Years,* p.142.

6   Hubert Butler, *In the Land of Nod,* p.30.

7   Ibid.

8   *Catholic Mind,* vol. iii, no. 3, March 1932, p.56.

9   The Fr Brown and Fr Corcoran quotations are taken from Brian P. Murphy, *The Catholic Bulletin and Republican Ireland,* pp.281-282.

10   Military Archives 2/46439.

11   *The Irish Times,* 19 April 1952, p.17.

12   Cooney, Dudley Levistone, 'Methodism: A woman's faith, a personal view', *Bulletin of the Wesley Historical Society in Ireland,* Vol. 13, 2007/8, pp.30-31.

13   Ibid.

14   Roddie, Robin Parker, *Register of Irish Methodist Preachers* (unpublished), p.C19.

Bibliography

Archdeacon, Matthew, *Shawn na Soggart* (Dublin, James Duffy, 1844)

Beckett, J.C., *The Anglo-Irish Tradition* (Belfast, Blackstaff Press, 1976)

Bennett, R.J., *Seán na Sagart: The Priest Hunter* (Dublin, Catholic Truth Society, 1949)

Blanshard, Paul, *The Irish and Catholic Power* (London, Verschoyle, 1954)

Boycott, Charles A., *Boycott* (Ludlow, Carbonel, 1997)

Bowen, Desmond, *Souperism: Myth or Reality* (Cork, Mercier Press, 1970)

Brown, Stephen, *A Guide to Books on Ireland* (Shannon, Irish University Press, 1919)

Brown, Stephen, *Ireland in Fiction* (Dublin, Hodges Figgis, 1912)

Brown, Stephen, *Libraries and Literature From a Catholic Standpoint* (Dublin, Browne and Nolan, 1937)

Brown, Terence, *A Social and Cultural History 1922-2001* (London, Fontana, 1990)

Butler, Hubert, *In the Land of Nod* (Dublin, Lilliput Press, 1996)

Carter, Carolle, *The Shamrock and the Swastika* (Palo Alto, Pacific Books, 1977)

Coogan, Tim Pat, *Michael Collins* (London, Hutchinson, 1990)

Cooney, Dudley Levistone, 'Methodism: A woman's faith, a personal view', *Bulletin of the Wesley Historical Society in Ireland*, Vol. 13, 2007/8

Daly, Mary E., *The Buffer State: The Historical Roots of the Department of the Environment* (Dublin, IPA, 1997)

Davitt, Michael, *Leaves from a Prison Diary* (Shannon, Irish University Press, 1972)

Ervine, St John, *Craigavon: Ulsterman* (London, Allen & Unwin, 1949)

Fanning, Bryan, *The Quest for Modern Ireland: The Battle of Ideas 1912-1986* (Dublin, Irish Academic Press, 2008)

Ferriter, Diarmaid, *Judging Dev* (Dublin, Royal Irish Academy, 2007)

Ferriter, Diarmaid, *Lovers of Liberty? Local Government in 20th Century Ireland* (Dublin, National Archives, 2000)

Foley, Dermot, 'A Minstrel Boy with a Satchel of Books' in *Irish University Review* Autumn 1974 (Shannon, Irish University Press, 1974)

Foster, R.F., *The Irish Story* (London, Allen Lane, 2007)

Foster, R.F., *Modern Ireland 1600-1972* (London, Allen Lane, 1988)

Grimes, Brendan, *Irish Carnegie Libraries* (Dublin, Irish Academic Press, 1998)

Jordan, Anthony J., *W.T. Cosgrave 1880-1965: Founder of Modern Ireland* (Dublin, Westport Books, 2006)

Kennedy, Michael, *Division and Consensus* (Dublin, IPA, 2000)

Keogh, Christina, *The County Library System in Ireland 1929* (Wexford, LAI, 1929)

Keogh, Christina, *Report on Public Library Provision in the Irish Free State, 1935* (Athlone, LAI, 1936)

Keogh, Dermot, *The Bishops and Irish Politics 1919-39* (Cambridge, Cambridge University Press, 1986)

Keogh, Dermot, *Ireland and the Vatican* (Cork, Cork University Press, 1995)

Keogh, Dermot, *Twentieth-Century Ireland: Nation and State* (Dublin, Gill and Macmillan, 1994)

Keogh, Dermot, *Twentieth-Century Ireland: Revolution and State Building* (Dublin, Gill and Macmillan, 2004)

Kerrigan, Gene, *This Great Little Nation* (Dublin, Gill and Macmillan, 1999)

Larkin, Felix (ed.), *Librarians, Poets and Scholars* (Dublin, Four Courts, 2007)

Lee, J.J., *Ireland 1912-1985: Politics and Society* (Cambridge, Cambridge University Press, 1990)

Library Association of Ireland, *Report of the Executive Board Oct. 1928-Apr. 1929* (Wexford, LAI, 1929)

Luce, J.V., *Trinity College Dublin: The First 400 Years* (Dublin, TCD Press, 1992)

Lyons, F.S.L., *Culture and Anarchy in Ireland* (Oxford, Oxford University Press, 1979)

Maguire, Martin, *Servants to the Public: A History of the Local Government and Public Servants Union 1901-1990* (Dublin, IPA, 1998)

Martineau, Harriet, *Letters from Ireland* (ed. Glenn Hooper) (Dublin, Irish Academic Press, 2007)

McMahon, Paul, Servants to the Public: A history of the Local Government and Public Servants Union 1901-1990 (Dublin, IPA, 1998)

Meenan, James, *George O'Brien* (Dublin, Gill and Macmillan, 1980)

Moffitt, Miriam, *The Church of Ireland Community of Killala & Achonry, 1870–1940* (Dublin, Irish Academic Press, 1999)

Moran, Gerard, 'Church and State in Modern Ireland: The Mayo County Librarian Case 1930-1932' in *Cathair Ma Mart*, 1987 (Westport, Westport Historical Society, 1987)

Murphy, Brian P., *The Catholic Bulletin and Republican Ireland* (Belfast, Athol Books, 2005)

Neligan, David, *The Spy in the Castle* (London, Prendeville Publishing, 1999)

O'Callaghan, Margaret, 'Language, Nationality and Cultural Identity in the Irish Free State', *Irish Historical Studies*, vol. 24, no. 94, p. 235

O'Halpin, Eunan, *Defending Ireland: The Irish State and its Enemies Since 1922* (Oxford, Oxford University Press, 1999)

O'Halpin, Eunan, *Spying on Ireland* (Oxford, Oxford University Press, 2008)

Ó Súilleabháin, Seán, *Leabharlann Chontae Liatroma 75 Blian ar an Saol* (Leitrim, Leitrim County Library, 2005)

Owens, Rosemary, *A Social History of Women in Ireland 1870-1970* (Dublin, Gill and Macmillan, 2005)

Puirseil, Niamh, *The Irish Labour Party 1922-73* (Dublin, UCD, 2007)

Quinlivan, Aodh, *Philip Monahan: A Man Apart* (Dublin, IPA, 2006)

Redmond, Brigid, 'In the Middle of the County Mayo: Organising the Library', *Capuchin Annual 1932* (Dublin, 1932)

Robinson, Lennox, *Curtain Up* (London, Michael Joseph, 1942)

Roche, Desmond, *Local Government in Ireland* (Dublin, IPA, 1982)

Rockett, Kevin, *Irish Film Censorship* (Dublin, Four Courts Press, 2004)

Smyth, Sheamus, *Off Screen: A Memoir* (Dublin, Gill and Macmillan, 2007)

Van Slyck, Abigail A., *Free to All: Carnegie libraries and American culture 1890-1920* (Chicago, University of Chicago Press, 1998)

Walsh, Roísín, 'Libraries', *Saorstát Éireann Official Handbook*, 1932 (Dublin, Talbot Press, 1932)

White, J.H., *Church and State in Modern Ireland 1923-1970* (Dublin, Gill and Macmillan, 1971)

Index